Habits for Resilient Learners

WHAT YOUR COLLEAGUES ARE SAYING . . .

Habits for Resilient Learners offers practical strategies that educators can immediately apply to help students build agency, perseverance, and confidence. The authors combine research, real stories, and classroom-ready tools to make resilience both teachable and attainable. This book is a valuable resource for anyone committed to preparing learners for success in school and in life.

Peter DeWitt, Ed.D., Instructional Leadership Collective, author

Habits for Resilient Learners by Prendergast, Lee, and Brueggeman invites educators to view resilience not as a fixed trait but as a skill that can be developed. In today's turbulent times, this perspective feels especially urgent. Each chapter highlights a specific habit, blending research with practical strategies that teachers can use right away. I value how the book grounds resilience in both evidence and classroom application, making it a resource that any teacher can lean on to build stronger connections with students and help them thrive as learners over the long term.

Diane Sweeney, author of *The Essential Guide for Student-Centered Coaching and Student-Centered Coaching: The Moves*

Habits for Resilient Learners is a must-read for every educator committed to preparing students for success in and out of school. In times of constant change and unforeseen challenges, resilience is no longer optional; it is a fundamental skill. Each chapter provides opportunities for reflection, allowing educators to pause, examine their own practices, and consider how to best support the growth of resilience in their students. *Habits of Resilient Learners* is grounded in evidence-based research and provides powerful insights for fostering perseverance, building confidence, and cultivating resilience in all learners.

Joy Casey, instructional coach,
Padilla Elementary, 27J Schools

Habits for Resilient Learners illuminates a powerful blend of lived classroom stories, clear research, and ready-to-use strategies that teachers can immediately integrate into practice. The learning from this book becomes the thread that weaves together how educators can support students in mastering content while building resilience.

Michael Nelson, thought partner,
Instructional Leadership Collective

Students need tools to help them succeed and teachers need practical strategies to help their students thrive. This dynamic team of experienced educators offers us an innovative approach to doing both. Not only do the authors share specific ways we can support students' academic success, they include strategies for promoting well-being too. A must-read for busy teachers who are ready to motivate their students to embrace their own learning journeys.

Carol Pelletier Radford, author of *Be a Legacy Teacher: Five Purpose-Filled Pathways for Late Career and Retiring Educators*

This book is a powerful resource for educators, offering research-based routines and habits that are easy to implement in everyday teaching. I feel confident that the student learning and student engagement in the classroom will be improved when these habits and tools are applied in practice. I especially appreciate the focus on healthy digital boundaries and fostering resilience in both educators and students—timely and transformative guidance!

Lindsay Deacon, senior instructional coach, author

From the very start of *Habits for Resilient Learners*, I could tell I would be shifting my personal and professional mindset. As a mother and educator, I learned ways to promote my own children and students not just to learn but to own their learning. Each new habit helped me to better understand and put into practice learning opportunities that prepare resilient learners to be successful in the school setting and beyond. The text offers practical and useful ways for any area or level of educator to take back. What a gift!

Andi Swantner, reading specialist, Wentzville School District

Habits for Resilient Learners by Prendergast, Lee, and Brueggeman delivers practical classroom strategies that support the development of resilient learning habits that lie within each of our students. Supported by research, the authors provide easy-to-implement tools and use relatable classroom experiences that teach how resilience is about moving beyond our struggles. When these 10 habits are modeled, reinforced, and prioritized by educators, they have the capability to impact learners well into their adult lives.

Sarah Moore, reading specialist,
Peine Ridge Elementary School

Habits for Resilient Learners

Empowering Students to Thrive Through Challenge and Change

Lindsay Prendergast
Piper Lee
Amanda Brueggeman

CORWIN

CORWIN

FOR INFORMATION:

Corwin
A Sage Company
2455 Teller Road
Thousand Oaks, California 91320
(800) 233-9936
www.corwin.com

Sage Publications Ltd.
1 Oliver's Yard
55 City Road
London EC1Y 1SP
United Kingdom

Sage Publications India Pvt. Ltd.
10th Floor, Emaar Capital Tower 2
MG Road, Sikanderpur
Sector 26, Gurugram
Haryana - 122002
India

Sage Publications Asia-Pacific Pte. Ltd.
18 Cross Street #10-10/11/12
China Square Central
Singapore 048423

Vice President and Editorial Director: Monica Eckman
Executive Content Leader: Liz Gildea
Content Development Editor: Melissa Rostek
Associate Content Development & Operations Manager: Zack Vann
Production Editor: Neelu Sahu
Copy Editor: Colleen Brennan
Typesetter: C&M Digitals (P) Ltd.
Proofreader: Lawrence Baker
Cover Designer: Candice Harman

Library of Congress Control Number: 2025048055

Paperback ISBN: 978-1-0719-9862-5

This book is printed on acid-free paper.

MIX
Paper | Supporting responsible forestry
FSC
www.fsc.org
FSC™ C013985

Printed in the United Kingdom
by Henry Ling Limited

26 27 28 29 30 31 10 9 8 7 6 5 4 3 2 1

Contents

online resources

Visit the companion website at
http://companion.corwin.com/courses/resilientlearners
for downloadable resources.

Foreword

Every generation of learners grows up in a different world, but none have experienced change at the pace of this one. Whether they're learning to read in kindergarten or preparing for college essays in high school, today's students are growing up in a world where information travels faster than reflection, where attention is a scarce resource, and where adaptability and resilience have become as essential as knowledge itself.

In a single day, a student might wake up to the glow of a phone or tablet, swipe through a loosely curated feed of news, entertainment, and information, and take in more content before leaving for school than most people once encountered in a week. At school, they learn from teachers, adaptive learning platforms, and now even AI tools that can explain, summarize, or solve nearly anything in seconds. After school, they move between gaming chats, group texts, YouTube tutorials, and social media feeds. Each moment in a student's day adds to an ongoing lesson, the kind that teaches, persuades, entertains, and compares, often without their awareness.

They can become experts in topics that once took years to explore. They can create, connect, and collaborate in ways we never imagined—and that kind of access can change how students experience learning. When answers come instantly, struggle can feel unnecessary. When every question can be solved with a quick search, the process of learning can lose its weight. I was reminded of this recently while observing a third-grade math lesson.

Students were working to solve multistep word problems about the mass of different objects, applying their understanding of multiplication and measurement. The teacher was clear and followed the lesson plan with precision. Yet as soon as the students began working independently and challenge entered the equation, a pattern emerged. Hands shot up in hopes of being given the next step. A few students asked to go to the bathroom. Others glanced toward a classmate's notebook. Only a small handful persisted, rereading the problem, revisiting the example on the board, and carefully working their way through the steps.

It wasn't a lack of effort; the teacher was doing exactly what the curriculum asked. What was missing wasn't in the lesson plan, success criteria, or learning intention. It was something less visible but far more powerful: the habits for resilience that help students stay with a problem when it feels hard. The strategies that teach them how to get unstuck and engage in what my former colleague called the "fabulous struggle." The belief that challenge isn't a signal to stop but an invitation to think differently.

Not long after that observation, I began reading *Habits for Resilient Learners* and found myself nodding along, page after page. This book captures exactly what I had witnessed in that classroom—the need for explicit, intentional teaching of the habits that help students navigate challenge with confidence. Our students are bright, curious, and capable, but they are also growing up in a world that often rewards speed over depth, convenience over persistence, and perfection over process. That's what makes the work of this book so necessary. It equips educators with the tools and mindsets that transcend any one curriculum or standard, tools that help us teach not just content but also character, curiosity, and adaptability.

Habits for Resilient Learners helps teachers support students not just to survive but to thrive in today's complex learning environments. It offers clear, research-based, high-leverage strategies that build independence, reflection, and agency. It is a book for every learner, with examples that show what resilience and adaptability look like in many scenarios. These habits aren't innate; they're developed through consistent practice and purposeful teaching, becoming the foundation for success both in and beyond the classroom.

Over fifty years ago, Alvin Toffler wrote, "The illiterate of the 21st century will not be those who cannot read and write, but those who cannot learn, unlearn, and relearn." Even in 1970, he understood that adaptability would become the new literacy. More than half a century later, his words feel prophetic.

That's what this book is all about, helping today's learners, and the teachers who guide them, build the capacity to learn, unlearn, and relearn. To face change with curiosity instead of fear. To see challenge not as a barrier but as the beginning of growth. I have no doubt you'll also find yourself nodding along as you discover the habits and accompanying strategies that are so needed by the students we work with every day.

Meghan Hargrave
Education Coach & Consultant

Acknowledgments

AUTHORS' ACKNOWLEDGMENTS

First and foremost, we want to thank the people who have been our greatest cheerleaders from the very beginning—Piper's and Lindsay's parents; Piper's children; Amanda's nieces and nephews, along with her dad and siblings; Lindsay's husband, Pete; and Amanda's husband, Jay. Their patience, encouragement, and willingness to carry extra weight in our absence gave us the gift of time and space to bring this book to life. We could not have made this journey without their steady love and support.

We are also deeply grateful to the friends and colleagues who allowed us to share pieces of their lives within these pages. A heartfelt thank you to Ellen Eikel, Summer Turner, Joe and Dominic Perry, Jessica Hanks, Diane Nanney, Meredith Mayer, and the students of Maryville University for trusting us with their stories. Their openness brought depth and authenticity to the lessons we hope shine through in this book.

Finally, we owe much to the incredible team at Corwin, whose encouragement and belief in this work helped carry it across the finish line. A special thanks to the forces that led us to AVL, creating the very space where our partnership began. And to our thought partners—Lori Stollar, Joy Casey, and so many others—thank you for your wisdom, collaboration, and unwavering support throughout this process.

PUBLISHER'S ACKNOWLEDGMENTS

Corwin gratefully acknowledges the following reviewers for their contributions.

Mariah Lightle
Elementary Teacher, Otis School District
Otis, CO

Lori J. Stollar, Ed.D.
Pennsylvania ASCD Executive Director; Independent Consultant; Director of Curriculum & Innovation (retired), Littlestown Area School District
East Berlin, PA

Natalie Tasillo
Teacher, Prince William County Schools
Dumfries, VA

Charlene Vermilion
Principal, Kent School District
Kent, WA

Crystal Wash
Teacher, Principal, SEL Specialist, CERA Researcher
Chicago, IL

Lara Watkins
Literacy/Instructional Coach, Brevard Public Schools
Palm Bay, FL

About the Authors

Lindsay Prendergast, Ed.D. brings nearly two decades of experience in global education, where her roles have ranged from leadership coach to principal, consultant, and classroom teacher. As a senior leader with The Danielson Group and founder of EdHabits consulting (www.edhabits.com) with Piper Lee, she collaborates with districts, schools, and educators to promote equitable teaching and learning. Lindsay's work centers on leading systems change and advancing instructional leadership with practical and impactful insights. Recognized as an ASCD Emerging Leader and Champion in Education as well as an AAIE Fellow, Lindsay is an established thought leader who frequently shares her expertise on leadership development, growth-centered supervision, and assessment practices through ASCD, Learning Forward, Edutopia, AAIE, EARCOS, AMLE, Cognia, and more. She coauthored the bestselling *Habits of Resilient Educators: Strategies for Thriving During Times of Anxiety, Doubt, and Constant Change* (Prendergast & Lee, 2024) and *Habits of Resilient Leaders: Personal Practices That Drive Professional Impact* (Prendergast & Lee, 2025), as well as dozens of articles and manuscripts in the field of education. Driven by a commitment to impactful change and global competence, Lindsay's work empowers educators to navigate complex challenges, fostering environments where both teachers and students thrive. Lindsay holds a bachelor's degree from Wofford College, a master's degree in education leadership from Colorado Western State University, and a doctoral degree in education leadership from Wilkes University.

Piper Lee brings over twenty-six years of experiential wisdom in education, including teaching, administration, instructional coaching, and leadership development. Her dedication to enhancing student learning and teacher effectiveness drives her national work as an instructional leadership coach.

Piper has partnered with students, educators, leadership teams, and families across various contexts, including support for district leaders and principals in one of the largest school districts in the country. Post-pandemic, she coached more than eight superintendents and over forty-five principals alongside Lindsay Prendergast, dedicating extensive time to data analysis, facilitating professional learning communities, and classroom observations. These experiences shape her evidence-based approach and inform the purpose of this book.

Piper champions the philosophy that "rigorous relationships" are foundational to transformative school cultures and effective leadership. Piper holds a B.A. in elementary education, a master's in curriculum and instruction, and an education leadership certification from Winona State University.

Grounded in practical strategies and informed by deep field experience, Piper equips education leaders to navigate complexity and foster environments where both students and educators thrive.

Amanda Brueggeman, Ed.D., is an education consultant and author whose teaching career started in 2004, bringing more than twenty years of experience in the field. Her extensive background includes ten years as an elementary school teacher and later as an instructional coach. She also currently works as an adjunct professor in Maryville University's Education Department, instructing undergraduate preservice teachers, master's-level specialists, and doctoral students in the teacher leadership program.

Dr. Brueggeman, known by students as Dr. B, is deeply passionate about collective efficacy in working with students, teachers, mentors, instructional coaches, and school leaders. She provides professional learning for beginning teachers and new teacher mentors, drawing from her book *Student-Centered Mentoring: Keeping Students at the Heart of New Teachers' Learning* (2022). Additionally, she trains instructional coaches and principals across the country in Student-Centered Coaching. Her student-centered philosophy remains central as she fosters connections with all educators. Amanda obtained her teaching degree in elementary education from Southeast Missouri State University. She furthered her education with a master's degree in educational technology from the University of Missouri and earned her doctorate in teacher leadership at Maryville University.

Introduction

WHY THIS BOOK? WHY NOW?

Learning—like leading—is a deeply human endeavor, and for learners across every age group, it should be a meaningful, affirming experience. However, in today's turbulent educational climate, students face a mounting sense of disconnection and discouragement. Rapid technological change, pandemic-induced disruptions, widespread misinformation, and constant societal pressures have created an emotional and academic fog for many. Anxiety, apathy, and overwhelm are now frequent companions in the learning journey. Amid this complexity, teachers are doing more than instructing—they are guiding young people through uncertainty, disconnection, and stress.

Teaching in today's world is emotionally demanding. The stakes feel higher than ever, and yet so does the opportunity for meaningful change. While schools work hard to accelerate academic recovery and social-emotional growth, the reality is clear: traditional approaches to learning are insufficient for preparing today's students for a rapidly changing world. More than ever, learners need tools not just to "get through" school but to thrive in spite of its many challenges. They need a foundation for agency, purpose, and emotional stamina. In short, they need resilience.

This book exists to meet that urgent need. *Habits for Resilient Learners* offers a framework of research-backed habits that empower students to manage uncertainty, embrace challenge, and thrive in complex learning environments. The habits outlined in this book are designed to empower student growth, enhance academic outcomes, and foster well-being. Through relatable anecdotes and ready-to-use strategies, the authors speak directly to K–12 educators navigating the real pressures of today's schools.

This book also speaks directly to *learners*. The habits are designed to enable teachers to help them build self-awareness, guiding them to understand what resilient learners do—and how they can do it, too. These approaches support students in developing essential skills like problem-solving, goal-setting, and self-regulation, while encouraging them to see challenges as opportunities for growth, not signs of failure. These are not just life skills—they are academic accelerators. When students practice these habits, they become more focused, motivated, and capable of navigating adversity in and beyond the classroom.

As authors, we bring decades of experience working alongside students, educators, and school leaders. We've coached learners struggling to find motivation, partnered with schools rebuilding their culture after trauma, and guided mentors working tirelessly to reignite a love of learning. This book distills those experiences—and the success stories that emerged—into a guide that honors both the vulnerability and strength required to grow as a learner today.

THE RESILIENCE IMPERATIVE: WHY LEARNING MUST CHANGE

The challenges students face today are real and varied. Academic disruption, heightened social-emotional demands, uncertainty about the future, and pressure from digital media all contribute to a fragile sense of self and success. In many classrooms, students are told what to do without being shown how to engage with learning as a reflective, empowering process. Many learners struggle to define their goals, understand feedback, manage stress, or connect to a deeper "why" behind their schoolwork.

We believe it's time to change that. The habits outlined in this book center around the core belief that students deserve tools for sustainable, holistic success. These are not quick fixes or motivational slogans. They are replicable practices rooted in cognitive science, positive psychology, culturally responsive teaching, and student-centered mentorship.

Resilient learners are not just more successful in school; they are better prepared for life. They are more adaptable in the face of change, more capable of healthy collaboration, and more confident in navigating academic and personal adversity. This is not to say that resilience is innate. On the contrary, resilience is learned. Like a muscle, it grows with intentional, repeated practice. By building this muscle through clear, actionable habits, we help learners shift from a passive mindset to one of curiosity, purpose, and growth.

HOW DO HABITS SUPPORT RESILIENT LEARNING?

Habits shape our automatic responses to the world. For learners, those automatic responses—how they handle feedback, manage frustration, collaborate with peers, or set personal goals—can determine whether they disengage or rise to the challenge. As educators, we've observed a powerful truth: learners flourish when they have structure, strategies, and belief systems that support them in moments of uncertainty. These become the habits for resilient learners.

For example, when a student understands how to set goals that reflect personal meaning (Chapter 4), they are more likely to persist in the face of difficulty. When they build confidence in their ability to give and receive feedback (Chapter 5), they become more open to growth. When they experience the strength of learning collaboratively with peers (Chapter 3), they develop a sense of shared purpose and belonging.

Each chapter in this book is designed around one such habit. As shown in Figure 0.1, these habits are interconnected, drawing from social-emotional, cognitive, and academic domains to form a comprehensive model of resilience. Some focus on internal mindset and identity, while others emphasize interpersonal relationships and external structures that support learning. Together, they cultivate not only stronger learners but also more confident human beings.

FIGURE 0.1 ● The Habits for Resilient Learners

WHAT READERS WILL FIND IN EACH CHAPTER

Every chapter in *Habits for Resilient Learners* begins with a real story—a glimpse into the life of a student or teacher confronting a challenge many will recognize. From these lived moments, we draw out a specific habit that could help that learner, and many others like them, not just cope but succeed.

Each habit is

- grounded in clear, accessible research,
- illustrated through authentic classroom experiences,
- supported by practical tools for instruction,
- designed for easy integration into daily practice, and
- aligned with social-emotional learning, academic performance, and equity goals.

HOW TO USE THIS BOOK

The habits described in this book are not sequential steps in a curriculum. Rather, they are interrelated practices that may be introduced individually, explored collectively, or revisited over time. You may choose to focus on one chapter at a time based on the needs of a learner, a small group of learners, or a classroom. Alternatively, you may work through the book as a study group of educators, using the "Pause and Reflect" and "Let's Reflect" sections to engage in deeper dialogue.

In each chapter, you will find a section that supports partnering with students and families. Making the connection to home and family support is essential to reinforcing habits for resilience. You will find questions that can be adapted to promote reflective dialogue with students and families. Taking these opportunities allows you to work with students and families to create a consistent message about the importance of self and social awareness. Parent workshops and newsletters are some of the ideas to use these questions in promoting further use of each habit. Open communication between teachers and families can ensure that students receive consistent support in developing these crucial skills.

However you determine to engage in these learning experiences, *Habits for Resilient Learners* will be more than a resource—it's a companion. It provides . . .

- a framework for integrating resilience-building into everyday teaching,
- activities and routines that support mental health and well-being,
- a roadmap for creating positive learning environments rooted in trust, and
- a toolkit to prepare students for academic and life success.

Here's a closer look at what each habit offers.

CHAPTER 1: NURTURE CORE BELIEFS

This chapter helps teachers support students in developing a positive sense of identity and self-efficacy. Students who believe in their ability to learn are more willing to take risks and persevere. Educators will discover how to cultivate affirming language, provide supportive feedback, and create an environment where belief in one's potential becomes the foundation for growth.

CHAPTER 2: CLARIFY STUDENT SUCCESS

Success means different things to different students. This chapter explores how teachers can guide learners to define success in ways that are personally meaningful and motivating. Through intentional conversations and goal-aligned tasks, students build a stronger sense of purpose and are better equipped to measure progress on their own terms.

CHAPTER 3: MOVE FROM GROUPS TO TEAM COLLABORATION

Many students have been placed in groups, but few have experienced true teamwork. This habit teaches how to foster collaborative learning communities where students take ownership, rely on one another, and feel accountable to a shared goal. Teachers will find tools to move beyond compliance toward authentic, inclusive collaboration.

CHAPTER 4: EMPOWER LEARNERS THROUGH GOAL-SETTING

Goal-setting becomes transformational when learners connect their personal motivations to their academic progress. In this chapter, the authors offer step-by-step guidance to help teachers coach students in setting meaningful, manageable goals. These strategies give students a roadmap for growth and a reason to keep going when things get hard.

CHAPTER 5: NAVIGATE THE FEEDBACK PROCESS

Feedback is a powerful tool for growth only when students know how to receive and apply it. This chapter equips educators with routines and language that help learners reflect, revise, and take ownership of the feedback process. The result? More confident, independent learners who embrace feedback instead of avoiding it.

CHAPTER 6: PERSEVERE THROUGH OBSTACLES

This habit is about grit with heart. Students will inevitably face setbacks, but their response can be shaped by what the classroom teaches. Teachers will explore how to normalize struggle, celebrate effort, and guide students in developing persistence. The strategies here help learners understand that challenge is not the enemy of learning—it's the engine of it.

CHAPTER 7: EMBRACE VULNERABILITY

When students feel safe enough to ask questions, admit confusion, and share ideas, real learning happens. This chapter focuses on cultivating a classroom culture rooted in psychological safety. Teachers will discover how to model vulnerability, invite authentic inquiry, and help students reframe mistakes as stepping stones, not setbacks.

CHAPTER 8: DEVELOP TECH-SAVVY SCHOLARS

Technology is everywhere, but digital fluency and discernment must be taught. This habit guides educators in helping students use technology with purpose, balance, and critical thinking. With strategies to foster digital citizenship and manage distractions, teachers can develop students who are not just users of technology but thoughtful, tech-savvy scholars.

CHAPTER 9: HARMONIZE MULTIMODAL LEARNING

Learning engages the whole body and brain. This chapter explores how teachers can leverage movement, visuals, sound, and emotion to activate deeper learning and focus. From flexible seating to embodied routines, this chapter offers creative strategies to help students regulate energy, increase engagement, and internalize learning through multiple modes.

CHAPTER 10: CULTIVATE RESILIENT LEARNING HABITS

This final chapter ties everything together. Resilience isn't a one-time response—it's a system of habits built over time. Teachers will learn how to create learning environments where students regularly practice reflection, agency, and adaptive problem-solving. These habits ensure students leave not only more skilled but more ready for life beyond the classroom.

You may recognize many of these ideas as best practices in teaching and learning. What makes this book unique is how we've anchored them to personal growth and resilience. The habits are not stand-alone tips but components of a holistic system that supports academic success and lifelong well-being.

LET'S GROW TOGETHER

Our invitation to you is this: don't read this book alone. Whatever your role in education may be, or no matter your years of experience, the learning becomes deeper when shared. Talk about it with a friend, journal about it with a group, apply the strategies in a coaching session or family routine. Better yet, start a book study in your school or community.

Many of the tools in this book are available on the *Habits for Resilient Leaders* companion website for download. Visit **companion.corwin.com/courses/resilientlearners** to access those online resources.

Throughout this book, we offer tools to help you track your journey, reflect on your development, and apply your insights in real time. This is your opportunity to invest in your future and in the future of the learners you support.

START HERE, START NOW

We are so glad you're here.

In the pages ahead, you will discover that resilience is not something reserved for extraordinary students. It is something that can be cultivated in every learner, at every age, in every setting.

You don't need to change everything. You just need to start with one habit. Let's begin.

Get Ready. Set Your Intentions. Now Let's Grow!

Use this table to journal several learning intentions as you begin reading. You'll find opportunities to revisit them as you finish the chapters!

1.
2.
3.

CHAPTER 1

Nurture Core Beliefs

Meredith, a sixth grader, usually loved being at school. Missing a day felt like missing out on an adventure. This hadn't always been the case, though. She remembered the confusing fog that descended when fractions were introduced in math class. Her hand shot up constantly, a silent plea for help, and she leaned on her teacher and classmates for guidance. But something shifted. Slowly, practice became her ally. Each completed problem, each understood concept, was a small victory. Meredith developed a few simple mantras, little mental pep talks that fueled her love of learning, especially when faced with not knowing. When a problem stumped her, whether it was understanding a complex question or struggling to remember the steps, she'd take a deep breath and reread the instructions, then the question itself. And if the answer still eluded her? As long as it wasn't a test, it was OK to ask a peer or the teacher for help. Above all, she knew the secret: keep practicing because she believed she would eventually be successful.

WHY BELIEFS MATTER

A fundamental aspect of resilient student learners is their belief in themselves. Learning is more than just a cognitive process; it is deeply intertwined with beliefs. Those beliefs are dependent on success and challenges. "The beliefs we hold are the cornerstone of what you say and the actions you take" (Brueggeman, 2022, p. 1). What any student believes about themselves as a learner, the concept of learning, and the world shape their willingness to learn. Research consistently demonstrates a strong correlation between high self-efficacy and increased motivation, persistence in facing challenges, ability to work with peers, and improved academic success. Self-efficacy is a strong predictor of academic success because it affects students' motivation, learning strategies, and resilience in the face of challenges (Bandura, 1997).

The key concept of self-efficacy is an individual's belief in their capability to succeed at a specific task or achieve a particular goal (Bandura, 1997). Learners who believe in their abilities are more likely to set challenging goals as well as persist when setbacks occur. Obstacles are viewed as temporary challenges rather than barriers because these learners actively seek out and use strategies that enhance their understanding. Resilient learners also manage stress and anxiety with more confidence and control. Low self-efficacy can have detrimental effects on student learning. Students with low self-efficacy are more likely to avoid challenging tasks, fearing failure and limiting their opportunities for growth. They may also give up easily when faced with obstacles, lacking the resilience to persevere. If students let it, negative beliefs associated with low self-efficacy will create a cycle of anxiety and self-doubt, significantly impacting their performance and producing a decline in academic success. When teachers know what characteristics to make a note of, it helps them understand how to better promote student self-efficacy (Figure 1.1).

FIGURE 1.1 • Characteristics of Self-Efficacy

STUDENT SELF-EFFICACY IS . . .	STUDENT SELF-EFFICACY IS NOT . . .
• Believing in one's ability to learn.	• Having a general feeling of self-worth or self-esteem.
• Putting in the effort.	• Possessing fixed traits.
• Being willing to persist when faced with challenges.	• Guaranteeing success.
• Setting and revising goals.	• Believing in perfection.
• Seeking a variety of strategies.	• Ignoring challenges or setbacks.
• Believing in one's competence in a subject or skill.	• Relying solely on luck or external factors.

All experiences, both positive and negative, profoundly shape our beliefs. "The major motivator for developing individual self-efficacy includes the enactive learning experience, experiences which allow the student to focus on their personal accomplishments and which are subject to mastery or evaluative criteria" (Hattie et al., 2021, p. 36). Positive experiences, such as overcoming challenges or receiving strengths-based feedback, can significantly boost self-efficacy and cultivate resilience. Conversely, negative experiences, such as repeated failures, criticism, or a lack of support, can erode self-efficacy and hinder the development of resilient learning habits. Recognizing the powerful impact of experiences is crucial for teachers and learners. By creating supportive and encouraging learning environments, we can cultivate positive experiences that foster strong self-efficacy and empower students to develop practical habits that will serve them throughout their lives.

The H.E.R.O. components, which stand for hope, efficacy, resilience, and optimism, are the basis of building habits for resiliency (Prendergast & Lee, 2024). "Hope is closely linked to efficacy and reflects a belief that you possess both the will and the way to achieve your goals" (pp. 166–167). It doesn't go without saying that you have to hope that positive outcomes will also occur. An optimistic learner will attribute their success on a project to putting in the hours and hard work of research. On the other hand, a pessimist will believe it is luck. It all comes together, as a scholar's likelihood of learning increases when they hope and believe that learning is achievable.

Self-efficacy is the beginning of developing resiliency and leads to many other influences. Increasing self-efficacy is intertwined with establishing collective efficacy, a group's belief in their ability to succeed. Educators Hollins-Alexander and Law (2022) share that we must first have self-efficacy as individuals: "When we truly believe our actions lead us closer to meeting our goals, we move closer to collective efficacy" (p. 140).

CONNECTION

You will read more about collective student efficacy and team-building in Chapter 3.

HELP STUDENTS EXPRESS THEIR BELIEFS

Understanding students' beliefs is crucial for effective teaching and learning. By providing opportunities for students to express their beliefs about themselves as learners, the nature of learning, and the world around them, educators can gain valuable insights into their students' perspectives and create a more supportive and inclusive learning environment. It is also essential to foster self-awareness and encourage students to reflect on their own learning processes and identify strengths and weaknesses. This leads to a stronger classroom community that is safe for students to share thoughts and perspectives with peers.

One key tool for helping students express their beliefs is the Beliefs Reflection Tool (Figure 1.2).

FIGURE 1.2 • Beliefs Reflection Tool

BELIEF STATEMENTS	SELF-ASSESSMENT RATING *1 = NEVER* *3 = SOMETIMES* *5 = ALMOST ALWAYS*	EXPLAIN YOUR REASONING
I believe I have the ability to learn.		
I can learn despite things that worry me.		
I am motivated to learn.		
I am willing to try new ideas or strategies.		
If I do not learn something the first time, I will try again.		
I want to work with others to learn.		
I think it is important to have conversations with others to learn.		
I like to observe others to learn more.		
I set and revise goals to help me learn.		
I am successful when I learn both content and skills.		

If this Likert rating reflection tool does not work for you or your student(s), you could try a different format, such as one or more of the following:

- **Questionnaire:** A set of carefully crafted questions that explore students' beliefs about learning, strengths and weaknesses as learners, goals for the year, and preferred learning styles

- **Journal prompt:** A series of prompts that encourage students to reflect on their learning experiences, identify challenges and successes, and articulate beliefs about themselves as learners
- **Class discussion:** Facilitated discussions where students share their perspectives on learning, discuss beliefs, and engage in respectful dialogue with peers

Completing the reflection tool or questionnaire a few times a year will allow learners to self-reflect on growth and changes. Setting up the process with norms that promote solution-based thinking will support students in any differences they showcase in their reflections. You can also promote metacognition by encouraging students to think about their thinking and develop strategies for increasing their confidence. Encouraging students to discuss self-reflections collaboratively and make connections to learning experiences will also foster student self-efficacy and help lead to collective student efficacy, which is essential in team-building.

As you engage with these reflections, consider how they connect to the Mindframes for Visible Learning. Specifically, the first learner's mindframe from the *Illustrated Guide to Visible Learning*: "I am confident that I can learn" (Hattie et al., 2024). A student who genuinely embodies this mindframe approaches the belief system with the expectation of success, always looking for opportunities to learn and grow. Conversely, a scholar who struggles with this belief may be hesitant to engage in learning, fearing failure and potentially limiting their learning potential. By understanding learners' beliefs, we can tailor our instruction and support to foster a stronger sense of confidence and empower learners to embrace the belief that they can learn and succeed.

PROMOTE AND REINFORCE STUDENT SELF-EFFICACY

Finding the right level of confidence matters significantly. As John Hattie and colleagues (2021) emphasize, embedding appropriate skills for a "Just Right" level of self-confidence is one of the "I" skills, a key component within a framework designed to connect to "we" skills, both of which lead to developing collective student efficacy. These "I" skills are not innate; they are cultivated. They include the essential beliefs of "I can," "I will," and "I see." These beliefs work in concert: "I can" fosters a sense of capability; "I will" instills determination and agency; and "I see" encourages a growth mindset, where students can visualize their progress and future success. By intentionally embedding these "I" skills into our instruction, we can help students maintain an optimistic outlook, believe in their capabilities, and develop a healthy sense of self-efficacy.

The most powerful way to build self-efficacy is through experiences of success. Design lessons and activities that allow students to master attainable tasks, working alongside them as need be. Take Diane, for example. Diane built strong relationships, and her students genuinely enjoyed being in her classroom. She took a natural approach and maintained high expectations for her students, encouraging them to think for themselves. Students can then gain confidence by observing others succeed, particularly their peers. Here are some ideas to promote mastery and vicarious experiences for learners:

- Share stories of successful students, both past and present.
- Encourage students to share their own successes and strategies with the class.
- Use the think-aloud strategy to model the belief process.

Read Diane's reflection on her experiences with students, which showcases some of these examples.

FROM THE LENS OF A TEACHER

How Diane Found Power in Connecting With Students

Diane reflects on her career, emphasizing the importance of fostering students' thinking skills. She dedicated extra time to working with students individually and in groups, even spending evenings reviewing their work. While this may seem like a considerable investment of extra time, Diane believes it was time well spent to truly understand her students and assist them in reaching their potential.

Gina is a memorable example of how taking the time pays off. Diane believes in building strong relationships with students, like Gina, whose writing improved significantly because she felt invested in by Diane. Diane created a supportive classroom culture through various methods, including Argus posters, celebrating mistakes, and read-alouds. She remembers crying in front of her students while reading Stone Fox. *She had to pause to collect herself, leaving her students staring at her, unsure of what to think, and some even started to cry!*

Teaching is hard, messy, and frustrating. However, Diane found that there is no greater gift than witnessing students' social and academic growth. Nothing compared to the love and pride of seeing them be confident in themselves. She stressed the importance of recognizing students' learning progress and providing tailored support.

Consider Diane's story to guide you in reinforcing students' core beliefs through relationship-building, which goes beyond the beginning of the year and requires authentic connections. This leads us to getting students to trust you, which sets the stage for other habits when building resilience. As Diane provided opportunities for students to reflect on both their successful experiences and their growth experiences, she offered feedback that emphasized effort and strategies while helping them set realistic and achievable goals. For example, instead of saying "You're smart," try "I can see how hard you worked on this project, and your resilience really paid off." Learners also benefit from visual reminders of building their encouraging belief system. Incorporate posters and sayings throughout your classroom. Whether content-specific or general, the goal is to create a classroom environment where students feel supported and encouraged to share their beliefs and to develop their academic identities. The sample student academic chart provided in Figure 1.3 serves as a tool to track progress and visually represent student growth based on their influencer, further reinforcing the "I can," "I will," and "I see" beliefs and contributing to a strong foundation of self-efficacy.

CONNECTION

Refer to Chapter 2 for more insights on how to weave social and emotional learning into academic instruction through meaningful learning objectives.

Offering scholars choices in their learning activities can also increase their sense of ownership and control, promoting self-efficacy. Research consistently demonstrates the positive impact of providing students with choice and autonomy in their learning. For example, allow them to select topics for research projects, choose from different methods for demonstrating their learning, or set their own learning goals. Furthermore, choice can be particularly beneficial for students from diverse backgrounds, as it allows them to select options that align with their cultural or individual learning preferences. This highlights

FIGURE 1.3 ● Sample Student Academic Identity Chart

INFLUENCER	AREA (CONTENT OR SKILL RELATED)	FEELING	INFLUENCER MESSAGE (POSITIVE OR NEGATIVE/ WORDS, ACTIONS, ETC.)	IMPACT ON IDENTITY
Example: Math teacher	Willingness to share answers in class	Safe space/take risks/OK if it is the wrong answer	"That's one way to consider that problem. Can you explain how you came up with that idea?"	I can share ideas in class without fear.
Reading teacher				
Classmate				
Coach				
Parent				
Sibling/friend				

Adapted from Prendergast and Lee (2024).

the critical point made by Carol Ann Tomlinson (2017) in *How to Differentiate Instruction in Academically Diverse Classrooms*:

> Kids of the same age aren't all alike when it comes to learning any more than they are alike in terms of size, hobbies, personality, or food preferences. . . . In a classroom with little or no differentiated instruction, only student similarities seem to take center stage. In a differentiated classroom, commonalities are acknowledged and built upon, and student differences also become important elements in teaching and learning." (p. 1)

When students have a say in what and how they learn, their motivation, engagement, and, ultimately, their self-efficacy will increase.

PRIORITIZE SELF AND SOCIAL AWARENESS

Developing strong self-efficacy is deeply intertwined with a student's understanding of themselves and their social world. Prioritizing self and social awareness is crucial for fostering this belief in one's ability to succeed. This involves cultivating self-awareness, self-management, social awareness, relationship skills, and responsible decision-making. The Collaborative for Academic, Social, and Emotional Learning (CASEL) provides a valuable framework for understanding and implementing social and emotional learning, highlighting these competencies as essential for academic success, positive social interactions, and overall well-being (CASEL, 2020). These skills play a vital role in building self-efficacy and developing resilience. Students who understand their emotions, recognize their strengths and weaknesses, and can manage their impulses are better equipped to navigate challenges and persevere in the face of setbacks.

The process of self-awareness begins with helping students understand their own emotions, thoughts, and values. It involves recognizing how these internal factors influence their behavior and interactions with others. Self-management builds upon this foundation, empowering students to regulate their emotions, manage stress, and adapt to different situations. Think back to Meredith: A student who recognizes the feeling of unease when faced with unknown questions can learn strategies like positive self-talk or rereading to manage that anxiety and continue to practice. Social awareness involves

FIGURE 1.4 ● Student Self-Awareness Reflection Tool

FOCUS AREA/GOAL	ACTIVITY/APPROACH OPTIONS	EXAMPLE CONTENT/PROMPTS
Introducing and Defining Core Concepts	• Guided discussion and brainstorming • Collecting and categorizing examples • Collaborative definition composition	• What does self-awareness look and sound like in and out of the classroom? • "Looks Like" (observable behaviors) and "Sounds Like" (internal thoughts/feelings expressed) • What does self-management look and sound like in and out of the classroom? • Compose definitions for self-awareness and self-management.
Facilitating Individual Self-Reflection	• Guided Activity: "My Awareness Journey"	• Select a tool: journals, notebooks, or choice reflection tools • What are some of my strengths? How do I know? • What are some things that trigger strong emotions in me (positive or negative)? • How do my actions impact others? • How do I communicate my needs effectively? • How can I develop my self-awareness skills further?
Consolidating Learning Through Class Discussion and Community-Building	• Facilitated Whole-Class Discussion	• What are some common challenges related to self-awareness and self-management? • What strategies can we use as a class to support each other's growth in these areas?
Notes and Action Steps:		

understanding the perspectives of others and empathizing with their feelings. Students with social awareness are more likely to build positive relationships, constructively resolve conflicts, and contribute to a positive school climate. Yet again, Meredith leaned on peers in appropriate ways and times. These skills are not taught in isolation; they are interwoven and build upon one another. A student with strong self-awareness is better positioned to develop social awareness, as they have a deeper understanding of their own reactions and how they might impact others. The Student Self-Awareness Reflection Tool, shown in Figure 1.4, provides options that aim to guide students in reflecting on their self-awareness and self-management skills, fostering a supportive classroom environment. Modify the reflection tool for your grade level, making adjustments to questions and activities as needed.

As a post-activity, find ways to develop peer mentoring opportunities. It is important to integrate regular opportunities for self-reflection throughout the year. This could be through journaling, check-ins, or other activities. Encourage students to apply their self-awareness and self-management skills in various classroom situations.

Educators can create a supportive environment where students feel safe, connected, and empowered by prioritizing awareness in the classroom. This focus on emotions and social awareness not only contributes to improved academic outcomes but also cultivates well-rounded individuals who are prepared to thrive in all aspects of their lives.

DEVELOP STUDENT RESPONSIBILITY

Further supporting students' beliefs in their actions leads to increasing student responsibility. It is crucial to help students take charge of their learning. This can be accomplished by uncovering how to accelerate a classroom's progression toward becoming independent learners. Based on Zaretta Hammond's (2015) work, independent learners are students who share the cognitive load, employ strategies to tackle tasks, and solve problems when needed. Encourage conversations and activities that showcase the learning characteristics students should embody. Start by having students visualize the sights and sounds of learning in their classroom and have them reflect using the questions listed in Figure 1.5.

FIGURE 1.5 ● Student Reflection Questions

QUESTION: WHAT DOES LEARNING LOOK LIKE?		
YOUNGER LEARNERS (~ UP TO SECOND GRADE)	**MIDDLE LEARNERS (~THIRD GRADE INTO MIDDLE SCHOOL)**	**OLDER LEARNERS (MIDDLE SCHOOL & BEYOND)**
• What happens when you learn something new? • Can you draw a picture of what learning looks like for you?	• Where do you learn best? (e.g., at a desk, on the floor, outside) • What tools or things help you learn? • Is learning always at school?	• What different ways can you learn? (e.g., reading, watching videos, doing experiments, discussing) • How do you know when you've learned something? • How does your learning style influence your approach to new material?
QUESTION: HOW DOES IT FEEL AS YOU ARE LEARNING?		
YOUNGER LEARNERS (~ UP TO SECOND GRADE)	**MIDDLE LEARNERS (~ THIRD GRADE INTO MIDDLE SCHOOL)**	**OLDER LEARNERS (MIDDLE SCHOOL & BEYOND)**
• What are some feelings you have when you learn something new? (e.g., happy, excited, confused) • Is it OK to feel confused sometimes?	• Describe how you feel when you're learning something challenging. • What helps you when you feel stuck or frustrated?	• How does your emotional state affect your learning? • What strategies do you use to manage frustration or confusion when learning? • How do you motivate yourself to learn, even when it's difficult?
QUESTION: HOW DO YOU EXPECT TO GET DIRECTIONS/INFORMATION? DOES A TEACHER ALWAYS GIVE YOU DIRECTIONS/INFORMATION?		
YOUNGER LEARNERS (~ UP TO SECOND GRADE)	**MIDDLE LEARNERS (~ THIRD GRADE INTO MIDDLE SCHOOL)**	**OLDER LEARNERS (MIDDLE SCHOOL & BEYOND)**
• How do you like to learn new things? (e.g., teacher telling you, looking at pictures, trying it yourself) Where else can you get information besides from your teacher?	• What are some different ways you can get information or directions? • Who else can you ask for help or information? (e.g., classmates, books, online resources)	• What are your preferred methods for receiving instructions and information? • How can you effectively seek clarification when needed? • How do you evaluate the reliability of different information sources?

QUESTION: CAN YOU PROBLEM-SOLVE BEFORE ASKING FOR HELP? IF SO, HOW?		
YOUNGER LEARNERS (~ UP TO SECOND GRADE)	**MIDDLE LEARNERS (~ THIRD GRADE INTO MIDDLE SCHOOL)**	**OLDER LEARNERS (MIDDLE SCHOOL & BEYOND)**
• What do you do when you get stuck? (e.g., try again, ask a friend, ask the teacher) • Can you think of one way to try to solve a problem before asking for help?	• What are some steps you can take to try to solve a problem on your own? • How do you decide when it's time to ask for help?	• What problem-solving strategies do you use? (e.g., breaking down the problem, brainstorming solutions, trying different approaches) How do you assess the effectiveness of your problem-solving efforts? • How do you know when it's appropriate to seek help, and how do you formulate your questions effectively?
QUESTION: HOW DO YOU FEEL IF YOU GET SOMETHING WRONG?		
YOUNGER LEARNERS (~ UP TO SECOND GRADE)	**MIDDLE LEARNERS (~ THIRD GRADE INTO MIDDLE SCHOOL)**	**OLDER LEARNERS (MIDDLE SCHOOL & BEYOND)**
• Is it OK to make mistakes? • What can you do if you make a mistake?	• What do you do when you get an answer wrong or make a mistake? • How can mistakes help you learn?	• How do you view mistakes and failures in the learning process? • How can you learn from your mistakes and use them as opportunities for growth? • How do you develop resilience in the face of setbacks?

Adapted from Brueggeman (2022).

Dependent learners are likely to possess a fixed or emerging mindset, whereas independent learners maintain a growth or innovator's mindset, where resilience is key in how to approach learning (Brueggeman, 2022). Independent learners are also more likely to be efficacious as they possess the skills and mindset to take ownership of their learning. Hammond's (2015) distinction between independent and dependent learners is relevant here and can be used to start discussions with scholars. Figure 1.6 shows potential responses to the

CONNECTION

In Chapter 6, you will learn more about cultivating a growth or innovator's mindset, leading to deeper work with student independence.

questions asked in Figure 1.5 about learning and demonstrates the characteristics of dependent and independent learners.

FIGURE 1.6 • Student Reflection Responses: Dependent vs. Independent Learner

IF A STUDENT RESPONDS, . . .	IF A STUDENT RESPONDS, . . .
• I listen and wait for the teacher to give information and directions. • I am unsure of how to start a new task. • I need support/scaffolds to complete a task. • When I get stuck, I will wait for help. • I have trouble remembering information or don't understand it most of the time.	• The teacher facilitates learning and/or sometimes gives information/directions. • I can read, research, or watch videos to obtain information. • I will use strategies/processes when starting a new task or try attempting a task first. • I have strategies for helping me get unstuck. • I remember most information/details or I know how to retrieve them from my long-term memory.
Then they are a DEPENDENT LEARNER.	Then they are an INDEPENDENT LEARNER.

Adapted from Hammond (2015).

Choice and ownership surface yet again. Fostering student independence hinges on providing opportunities for student voice and control over their learning. This is particularly relevant when considering learners' beliefs about being able to read. As researcher Jeff Wilhelm emphasizes, these beliefs are complex, diverse, and deeply intertwined with their views on learning. In their work with adolescent boys, Wilhelm and Smith (2014) observed that control plays a crucial role in reading independence. As they note, "The boys in our study also wanted to exercise control over their reading. Indeed, some of them went so far as to say that it's not the book so much that fosters enjoyment but rather the power to choose the book" (p. 274). This highlights the importance of offering students, especially boys, agency in their reading choices to cultivate a sense of ownership and greater engagement with literacy.

Pause and Reflect

How can you encourage conversations and activities that showcase the learning characteristics students should embody?	
What are the responses and behaviors your students exhibit in connection to dependent and independent learners?	
How can you foster student independence and provide opportunities for student voice and control over their learning?	

Developing student independence is built from strong teacher-student connections. Self-regulation techniques, combined with the support system fostered by strong teacher-student connections, empower students to become more independent learners. When teachers encourage peer collaboration, it also allows students to learn from each other, as seen in Dominic's science class example. Dominic's perspective showcases how he feels comfortable seeking help and taking ownership of learning because of his rapport with specific teachers.

FROM THE LENS OF A STUDENT

Dominic's Take on Building Student Independence

Dominic, a middle schooler, shared that learning had typically been easier for him from those he felt connected to, like friends or family. However, his math and science teachers were working to build connections and rapport in order to build more independent students. He noted that his math and science teachers made those connections by discussing shared interests during the first week of class, focusing on getting to know the students, which laid the groundwork for future interactions. Dominic also described how the math and science teachers allowed students to ask friends or watch videos independently before approaching a teacher, demonstrating initial self-reliance. Dominic said that his science teacher set reasonable deadlines, which contributed to students managing their time effectively. He even mentioned his math teacher using calming videos with breathing exercises to help students manage test anxiety. Even small acts, like helping teachers with tasks and passing out papers, can strengthen the student-teacher bond and create a sense of shared responsibility.

When planning for independent learning, consider Hattie's "Diagnose, Intervene, and Evaluate" model (Hattie & Zierer, 2018). This process should be central to how we work *with* students to develop beliefs in their own independence. Effective independent learning isn't simply about giving students free rein; it requires careful consideration of their individual needs and learning profiles, with the added influence of social and cultural factors. Therefore, *diagnosis*, in this context, involves helping students understand their own strengths and weaknesses, as well as their beliefs about themselves as learners. *Intervention* involves co-creating independent learning tasks and activities with students that are tailored to their needs and beliefs. Adjustments also may need to be made along the way as we take time to see change and encourage students. Lastly, a range of *evaluation* methods can be provided through a collaborative process with learners. Simply asking questions like "What worked?" and "What didn't work?" using the self-reflections with this habit, as well as just talking with students, can all build resilience and independence. This repeated cycle of diagnosis, intervention, and evaluation ensures that independent learning is a strategic and impactful approach to fostering student belief in their capacity for independence rather than a haphazard journey.

STUDENT-FAMILY PARTNERSHIP REFLECTION

Fostering emotional intelligence at home involves helping children identify and name their feelings in multiple capacities. For example, if a teacher notices a student struggling with self-management in the classroom, they can communicate with the family to explore if similar challenges are present at home and work together to develop strategies. With these guiding questions, you can promote beneficial conversations with families by allowing them to share their own experiences and strategies, extending the sense of community and shared learning beyond the classroom.

- What is self-awareness and self-management?
- How do we manage emotions?
- What decisions do we make that are responsible and caring?
- How do we use what we learn about awareness at home and outside of school?

Another option is to embed these questions in a newsletter or weekly communication home. As you build each habit, you can incorporate more student-family reflective questions.

The Big Ideas

In this chapter, you explored the link between self-efficacy and resilience in students. As you apply the strategies around helping scholars build their self-efficacy, remember that fostering healthy self-confidence is essential. Independent learners are more resilient, so encourage student ownership of learning by providing opportunities to explore their beliefs, develop self-awareness strategies, and increase responsibility. Teaching clear communication of thoughts, feelings, and needs further strengthens relationships and support-seeking behaviors. Prioritizing self-awareness and management of learning creates a safe, connected, and empowering environment where resilient students thrive.

Let's Reflect

What is your current practice for prioritizing awareness and developing student responsibility? What would you like to change?

What resonated with you about supporting students' beliefs and developing healthy levels of self-confidence?

What do you hope to learn more about as it relates to building students' self-efficacy?

What's Next?

In Chapter 2, you will dive into purpose-driven learning and explore practical strategies for implementing vision-casting in diverse educational settings. This includes examining specific tools and techniques for helping students articulate their "why," fostering stronger teacher-student relationships, and developing effective methods to unlock learner passions and empower self-directed learning. We will also investigate how to assess the impact of these approaches on student motivation and engagement, along with how to unlock the purpose of learning intentions.

CHAPTER 2

Clarify Student Success

At the start of the lesson, just as they did every day, the students had pulled out their learning notebooks. Ms. Robertson had communicated the learning intentions for the math block, the "what" they were learning, and the "why" behind it. Deep into solving math word problems, Katelyn paused. Her notebook displayed the intention: "Identify the correct operation." Her hand-drawn lightbulb symbol beside it signified her understanding of its real-world problem-solving purpose. Connecting her current task about combining groups, she then drew a small triangle—her personal code for an activity, directly aligning with that day's intention. Across the room, Otis was working on a different problem. When asked by Ms. Robertson what he was working on at the moment, he pointed to the learning intention in his notebook with his pencil. Then, Otis shared the intention: "Represent problems visually." "After I complete a bar model for this problem, I'll add a square symbol, my code," Otis continued. This student-driven "coding" actively links their work to the learning intentions, illuminating the "what, why, and how" of their learning and making their academic journey visible. Ms. Robertson circulated, observing more tangible connections that foster deeper engagement and understanding.

THE IMPORTANCE OF CLARIFYING SUCCESS

Many educators and researchers have observed that students are not inherently burned out by learning itself, but rather by engaging in learning that lacks purpose. More than 2,500 years ago, Plato recommended that children learn "by what amuses their minds" instead of through force or rigidity. In this context, Theodora Bogiou (2025) emphasizes motivation, drawing on this timeless wisdom that aligns with contemporary views: the most effective educational settings are those where students grasp the personal significance of learning, develop confidence and emotional control, and feel a connection to their future beyond just the curriculum. This perspective highlights the crucial role of purpose in igniting motivation that leads to student success.

To foster genuine student success, we must expand our definition beyond mere grades or test scores. A richer understanding encompasses intrinsic motivation and long-term fulfillment, nurturing learners who are Knowledge-ABLE and Information-FULL (Hammond, 2024a). This success aligns with the CASEL framework's focus on students developing self-awareness skills, including identifying emotions; linking feelings, values, and thoughts; integrating identities; examining biases; experiencing self-efficacy; fostering a growth mindset; and nurturing a sense of purpose (CASEL, 2020). As Leh (2025) simplifies the CASEL framework in her resources, she lists those skills along with self-management abilities, such as setting personal and collective goals and demonstrating both personal and collective agency. The main tip she gives is to have resources, such as a poster or bookmark with the skills and tips, handy to use with and by students. Success, in this context, means becoming active participants in their learning, moving from dependent learning to independent learning, and developing their cognitive capacity.

A fundamental step in cultivating resilient learners who are engaged, motivated, and successful in meaningful ways is providing students with clarity in their learning. Clarity involves helping students understand the intention of what they are learning, why they are learning it, and how they know they learned it. Studies and research highlight the significant impact that when teachers are clear, students can better plan, predict, set goals, and judge their own progress (Hattie et al., 2024). Teacher clarity has an effect size of 0.85, which is over double the impact on students (Hattie, n.d.c) and includes the elements of learning intentions and success criteria. Researchers, along with Hattie, highlight that until now, our view and application of success criteria have been too limited, resulting in only 30 percent of students knowing how they have learned something (Almarode et al., 2021). Almarode and Vandas (2018) go on to highlight that fragmented teaching and learning, activity-driven instruction, misaligned strategies, lack of progress-monitoring of learning, and unhelpful assessment data are common aspects of the clarity problem.

While teachers must clearly communicate learning intentions and success criteria, clarity is a bi-directional process; learners must also engage with these components (Almarode et al., 2021).

Students need a clear understanding of what successful learning involves, using the criteria in Figure 2.1 as a guide and benchmark throughout their progress. A research study published by The New Teacher Project (TNTP, 2018) about the opportunity myth, found that students spent more than 500 hours per school year on assignments that were not appropriate for their grade level and with instruction that didn't ask enough of them. The report shares that although most students do what is asked of them and many even earn As and Bs, they only demonstrate mastery of grade-level standards on assignments 17 percent of the time. Focusing on the learning process, rather than just the outcome, is essential for igniting greater motivation and fostering a growth-oriented and innovative mindset. The "opportunity myth" in the TNTP study shows how students and families are misled into thinking that hard work and good grades guarantee post-graduation opportunities. Many graduates are unprepared, not due to incapability, but because they rarely had the chance to engage in challenging, grade-level work. This chapter explores purpose-based learning as a journey, not a destination, toward achieving successful learning clarity.

FIGURE 2.1 ● Characteristics of Student Success

CLARIFYING STUDENT SUCCESS IS . . .	CLARIFYING STUDENT SUCCESS IS NOT . . .
• Providing a clear understanding of what success looks like.	• Communicating learning intentions without learners engaging with them.
• Communicating learning intentions and their purpose.	• Struggling to articulate the learning purpose and process.
• Involving a bi-directional process with both teachers and learners.	• Using a narrow perspective and use of success criteria.
• Utilizing multiple approaches while interacting with the success criteria.	• Using methods that may not provide clarity.
• Taking ownership of the learning journey.	• Relying solely on the teacher to lead the learning.
• Making learning more visible and measurable.	• Limiting the results of the learning process and outcomes.

Furthermore, sharing your personal purpose as an educator can incite students' recognition that you care and potentially open pathways to stronger relationships (Prendergast & Lee, 2024). Strong relationships are a key entry point for promoting equitable actions and attitudes in education (Hubbard, 2023) while also fostering psychological safety and collaborative inquiry. Combining clear communication of learning intentions and success criteria with sharing purpose and building strong relationships provides a foundation for students to understand the "what, why, and how" of their learning and enables them to take ownership of their learning (Almarode, 2021). This intentional exploration, fueled by curiosity and responsible decision-making, together with an increasing sense of purpose, is essential for students to feel connected to their learning and future.

Pause and Reflect

How might redefining "student success" to include purpose, motivation, and ownership shift the way you design learning experiences in your classroom?

___

___

___

In what ways could you make learning intentions and success criteria more visible and meaningful so that students engage with them as active participants in their own learning journey?

___

___

___

ESTABLISHING A VISION FOR THE LEARNING JOURNEY

Uniting a school community around a shared vision is an impactful process that builds resilience. While school leaders involve stakeholders in formulating a vision for the whole system, teachers can employ similar vision-casting techniques in the classroom to collaboratively shape the learning experience with students. This process can significantly contribute to clarifying what student success looks like and setting the stage for resilient learners. When students feel their perspectives are invited and their ideas are valued and heard, they are likely to experience a sense of agency and ownership, as well as psychological safety within the classroom system, which contributes to their own resilience and the collective resilience of the group.

Consider the following steps to involve students in developing a clear vision for the learning journey in your classroom (Prendergast & Lee, 2025):

1. Inventory classroom values.
2. Design learner profiles.
3. Document the journey.

Begin by taking an inventory of the values present within your classroom community. This involves gathering perspectives from your students. Seek opportunities to synthesize the results and share them with the students. When sharing, hold back from immediately stating specific action steps or outcomes. Instead, let students process the information through your facilitation. Guide students toward narrowing the information into trends or patterns that encompass broader themes. Utilizing consensus-building tools or strategies can help elicit agreement regarding the shared values, beliefs, or philosophies that will guide the classroom community. These might be named shared agreements, value statements, or community beliefs.

Based on the values identified in step 1, an effective approach to casting a vision can be developing a clear and common understanding of what you aspire to observe as the effect of your efforts on the learners in your classroom. This could involve creating a "learner profile" that describes the characteristics of a successful learner within your classroom setting. Building upon the classroom values analysis, gather a comprehensive range of input from students about these desired characteristics. Consider what characteristics you hope students will embody by the end of the year or a specific learning unit. Collect a diverse range of ideas and compare them to established classroom values alignment. Once compiled, ensure consistent and ongoing communication of this learner profile within the classroom community.

The last part of the process is to examine and celebrate the learning journey by routinely asking students to describe their experience through the learning process in your classroom. This step entails gathering information directly from the students or learners themselves to illustrate their journeys through your unique classroom system or special learning experiences.

(Consider the need for confidentiality as a premise for this work.) Compare the students' described experiences with the classroom values inventory results and the learner profile. This offers another chance for triangulation, helping to confirm that the classroom's vision and aspirations are mirrored in the daily reality experienced by students. Celebrating milestones along the learning path or the successful navigation of challenges can also reinforce the sense of progress and resilience that the vision-casting process aims to cultivate. This practice can acknowledge their contributions to the collective classroom journey, serving as a powerful way to affirm the shared vision and the efforts made to achieve it.

The tool in Figure 2.2 provides a framework for you to reflect and implement a vision-casting plan for a learner profile with your classroom of students. As we uncover learners' motivations later in the chapter, you can couple this process with the additional option of students creating their own independent learner profiles.

UNCOVERING LEARNERS' MOTIVATIONS

Recognizing the true motivations of each student is essential for defining success and creating a flourishing learning space. By taking the time to discover students' motivations, teachers reveal significant avenues for engagement, resilience, and profound learning. This requires examining more than just surface participation and exploring the web of personal passions, goals, and the influence of relationships and real-world context. As Almarode and Vandas emphasize in *Clarity for Learning* (2018), when students can articulate what they are learning, why they are learning it, and how they will know that they have learned it, their sense of ownership and motivation increases. This clarity, however, extends beyond the immediate learning target; it encompasses a student's understanding of how learning connects to their personal world and future. There are three key ideas you can use to elevate your students' motivation to learn:

- Build and maintain strong teacher-student relationships.
- Foster a genuine passion for learning.
- Connect learning to students' aspirations and relevance in the world.

FIGURE 2.2 ● Classroom Vision-Casting Process Template

STEP	GUIDING REFLECTION QUESTIONS	KEY ACTIONS AND FOCUS AREAS	POTENTIAL EVIDENCE AND OUTCOMES
1. **Inventory Classroom Values:** Core Beliefs, Principles of the Classroom Environment and Interactions	• What are the most important values for a positive and productive learning environment? • How can I involve students in identifying and defining our shared classroom values? • How will these values be visibly represented and reinforced in our daily routines and interactions?		
2. **Design Learner Profiles:** Holistic View of ALL Students' Strengths, Interests, Learning Preferences	• What are the diverse academic strengths of each of my students? • What are their interests and passions? • What are their preferred learning styles and environments? • What social-emotional needs or challenges impact learning?		
3. **Document the Journey:** Capture Evidence of Growth, Challenges, and Achievements to Inform Future Practice and Celebrate Progress	• What methods will I use to track progress toward our classroom vision and values? • How will I document individual growth and challenges? • How can students be involved in documenting their own learning journey and reflection of progress? • How will we celebrate milestones and successes as a class and for individuals?		

Strong teacher-student relationships are foundational in this process, creating a trusting and supportive classroom community where students feel comfortable sharing their interests and goals. Think back to Chapter 1 and Diane's story of connecting with her students. We share personal experiences as a learner to connect with students, just as we would with our fellow educators across the hall or on a committee. Carrington (2019) states in her book, *Kids These Days*, that with all relationships, it comes down to "human connection." Take a trip down memory lane and consider both positive and negative memories—field trips, favorite projects, parent-teacher conferences, taking assessments, and others. Be intentional with sharing details appropriately, while still being authentic. When we share what was learned from those moments, it helps us relate to our students and builds a sense of trust and mutual respect (Brueggeman, 2022). You may also consider general stories that accompany content or activities as a way to connect with scholars. As author Angie Freese (2023) shares, "A story can draw the learner in and without much effort or consideration, soften the positional or authoritative space between you and your students" (p. 100). Above all, being present with students and striving to understand them greatly contributes to creating a trusting environment that encourages learning.

Fostering a genuine passion for learning requires more than just engaging activities; it involves tapping into students' intrinsic desires to understand and master new concepts. This can be achieved by providing choices in how students learn and demonstrate their understanding, thereby increasing their autonomy—a key psychological need linked to motivation. When learning experiences are designed to be active, allow for discovery, and connect to students' existing interests—no matter how specific, such as monster trucks for a young reader—the learning becomes more exciting and personally meaningful (Cullins, n.d.). Connecting learning to students' aspirations and its relevance in the real world offers a powerful "why" that can sustain motivation, particularly when tackling challenging content.

CONNECTION

In Chapter 4, you will dive deeper into goal-setting and explore how to help students be active participants in the reflective process and further enhance their focus and commitment to achieving academic success.

To support this work, consider having students create their own independent learner profiles that can accompany them throughout the school year and beyond. Helping students view themselves as capable learners by also setting realistic goals and celebrating the process rather than just the outcome further fuels this passion and develops what Almarode and Vandas (2018) refer to as learner agency and efficacy. Consider using Figures 2.3 and 2.4 as templates.

FIGURE 2.3 • Student-Created Learner Profile: Elementary Level

ALL ABOUT ME!		
Things I Love to Do: (drawing, playing outside, video games, reading, etc.)	Something I'm Good At:	Something I Find Tricky:
My Favorite Subject and Why:	When I Grow Up, I Want to Be:	My Favorite Recess Activity:
I Learn Best When:	I Get Excited to Learn When:	A Question I Have About the World Is:

FIGURE 2.4 • Student-Created Learner Profile: Secondary Level

MY LEARNER SNAPSHOT	
Current Interests/Hobbies:	Subjects I Enjoy and Why:
Subjects I Find Challenging and Why:	Dreams and Goals After High School:
Skills I Want to Develop:	My Preferred Learning Environment:
What Motivates Me to Learn?	Examples of How Current Learning Connects to My Future/Real World:

COACHING LEARNERS TO ARTICULATE ACADEMIC PURSUITS

How many of us often get the questions, "Why is this important to know, how is this going to help me later in life, or when will I ever use this?" Infusing teaching and learning with purpose begins with intentional planning for integration (Prendergast & Lee, 2024). It's not enough for educators to simply state what students will learn; fostering a deep understanding of why it matters can dramatically elevate engagement and ownership of the learning process. Involving students in this process takes motivation to a deeper level. Purpose-based learning is not a singular event but an ongoing journey toward achieving learning clarity and providing robust support for students. It's about fostering an environment where students continuously seek and understand the relevance of their educational experiences.

Research such as Jordan and Hawley's (2012) study demonstrates how grounding content in a clear and compelling purpose can significantly enhance student engagement and understanding. Their work suggests that when students in U.S. history, for example, understand that the purpose of their learning is to become informed and active participants in a democracy, they are more

FROM THE LENS OF A STUDENT

How Jaden Learned the Power of Purpose

In my fifth-period Controversial Studies class, we followed a structured outline: we were assigned a topic, given two weeks to write a cohesive argument supporting our opinion, and then presented it to the class. After our first round of essay submissions and presentations, Mr. Underburg, our teacher, had an important conversation with us about the purpose of these essays. From the start, Mr. Underburg emphasized the importance of respecting others' opinions and refraining from tearing each other down. However, in this discussion, he went deeper into explaining why we were doing this assignment. He clarified that the goal wasn't simply to share our thoughts or convince others that our opinion was the only right one. Instead, the purpose was to learn how to communicate our ideas effectively and persuasively while respecting differing viewpoints. This conversation completely changed how I approached the assignment. Before understanding the purpose, I focused on undermining opposing arguments, believing that was the key to winning my audience. After Mr. Underburg's clarification, I began acknowledging and addressing the validity of other perspectives in my writing. I made it a point to communicate respectfully and thoughtfully, and this shift significantly improved the quality of my work.

likely to connect with the subject matter on a deeper level and appreciate its relevance to their lives as citizens. This aligns with broader findings in the science of motivating young people. For example, David Yeager (2024) emphasizes that adolescents and young adults are particularly driven by a desire to find purpose and make a prosocial impact. On page 40, another student, Jaden, shares her perspective on the importance of purpose and how taking a purpose-based approach can shift the focus from merely completing tasks to a deeper, more student-driven engagement with the learning process. Ultimately this leads to a more meaningful and lasting understanding.

CONNECTION

In Chapter 3, you will gain ideas for how to transform a classroom of groups into teams, which can support how students share their ideas and skills in a purposeful way.

Encouraging students to share their perspectives, contribute to classroom discussions, and even help shape learning activities validates their experiences and insights, making them active partners in the educational process. As noted by Hattie (2012), clear learning intentions and success criteria are critical for student achievement, and student involvement in understanding and articulating the purpose amplifies this effect. In *Habits of Resilient Educators* (Prendergast & Lee, 2024), three key strategies for teachers are given: plan for purpose, communicate purpose, and share purpose. Figure 2.5 offers a reflective tool that embeds that process. Use it as you plan a lesson or activity to guide your integration of purpose to be more inclusive of students' perspectives.

CONNECTING LEARNING ACROSS LEVELS

Learning success happens in various ways and at unique times for each student. As Frey et al. (2018) share in their agreement with other learning researchers in *Developing Assessment-Capable Visible Learners*, learning occurs across phases—surface, deep, and transfer.

- **Surface Level:** Students focus on one idea at a time, whether concept or skill.
- **Deep Level:** Students see connections, relationships, and schema between ideas and learn to organize skills and concepts.
- **Transfer Level:** Students apply knowledge in increasingly new and novel situations.

Students who are assessment-capable are able to move through surface, deep, and transfer phases of learning more adeptly (Frey et al., 2018). Those on this path toward being assessment-capable have a clear understanding of what success means, both

FIGURE 2.5 • Integrating Purpose With Students

	TEACHER CONSIDERATIONS	STRATEGY FOR STUDENT INVOLVEMENT	STUDENT CONSIDERATIONS
Plan for Purpose Essential Question: How does this learning connect to larger concepts or real-world applications identified by both teachers and students?	• Why was this learning task identified as the best choice to use with students? • Why is this the most appropriate standard to teach at this time? • How might this knowledge or skill be valuable to students in their future: academic, personal, or professional?	Conduct a "Purpose Discovery" where students brainstorm potential real-world applications.	• How do you think understanding this might be useful now or in the future? • What problems in our community or the world could this learning help us address?
Communicate Purpose Essential Question: How can we explicitly articulate the "why" for a unit or project?	• How can I state not just what students will do or know, but what they will understand or be able to do as a result? • What examples, case studies, or problems illustrate the relevance of the learning in authentic contexts?	Incorporate a "Student-Generated Purpose Statements" activity where students work in groups to rephrase the learning intentions and purpose.	• What are some examples, or problems, that showcase how relevant the learning is in real-life contexts? • What ideas connect to interests or future aspirations?
Share Purpose Essential Question: How can we make the purpose visible and championed by both teachers and students?	• How can I prompt students to lead reflections on the overarching goals as they progress through a unit or project? • What formats (written, oral, visual) can students and I use to explain why what they are learning matters to others?	Implement "Purpose Ambassadors" or rotating roles where students are responsible for starting a lesson by reminding peers of the learning purpose and how it is being met.	• Who can I share my explanation with about why this learning matters? • What formats can I use to communicate the purpose to a broader audience?

during the learning journey and at its conclusion. This involves more than just a grade; it means understanding the specific skills, knowledge, and qualities being developed. Almarode and Vandas (2018) also highlight the importance of co-constructing learning intentions and success criteria with students, a practice that inherently gives students a voice and a stake in their educational journey. A powerful strategy for achieving clarity at all levels is to involve students in co-creating success criteria. This practice aligns with assessment for learning principles, where the goal is to use assessment to improve student learning rather than simply to measure it (Stiggins et al., 2006). Use the chart shown as the Pause and Reflect box that follows as a guide for planning to incorporate some of these practices.

FROM THE LENS OF A TEACHER

Jess Empowers Agency by Clarifying Learning With Students

Before learning progressions, teaching felt like driving blind for elementary teacher Jess. How could students navigate the path if they didn't know the destination? A game changer was unpacking learning progressions and making them student-friendly, clarifying the end goal for everyone. Getting students involved was also crucial. Jess and the students used worked examples, rating them 1 through 4 based on the progression stages, discussing why each earned its score and what could make it "level up" to the next stage. This provided a visible path to the learning outcomes.

Students then used these progressions to self-reflect on their own work. Jess remembers one student, who often struggled with frustration, intently comparing their draft to the leveled examples. Their face lit up as they realized, "Oh, I'm at a Level 2 because I need more details! I know what to do to get to Level 3!" For students with diverse learning needs, breaking down the goal into steps made "leveling up" achievable. This clarity also improved Jess's ability to work effectively with small groups. Ultimately, this shared understanding answers the question, "How do you know if you are successful or fluent at . . . ?"

Coaching learners effectively involves guiding them through reflective practices infused with their interests and goals, such as revisiting their student-created learner profile related to tasks. Self-assessment activities that link current learning to personal growth are also invaluable. Through reflection, students can create a narrative of their learning, understanding how tasks and subjects form a cohesive, meaningful picture.

CONNECTION

Refer to Chapter 5 for more insights on helping students learn about giving and receiving feedback.

Pause and Reflect

PAUSE AND REFLECT STRATEGY FOCUS	STRATEGY EXPLANATION	WHEN AND HOW CAN I INCLUDE STUDENTS IN THESE AREAS?
Communicate the Learning Intention	Examine and discuss the overall learning goal along with the purpose.	
Analyze a Range of Examples	Provide possible examples related to a task or project.	
Co-Create Success Indicators	What does it look like, sound like, and feel like to be successful with this task/topic?	
Categorize and Revise Success Criteria	Group similar ideas and refine the language to be student-friendly.	
Repeat and Refer Back to Criteria	Repeat the learning goal multiple times and continuously bring learners back to the success criteria.	
Celebrate	Recognize and share the steps and outcomes of the learning journey.	

Researcher John Sweller explains that this process supports germane load—the cognitive effort in developing schemas for long-term memory, crucial for deep learning and knowledge transfer (cited in Clark, 2025). Sweller also describes activities that help learners integrate new information with prior knowledge, strengthening their mental models. As you continue incorporating intentional use of learning intentions and success criteria with students, also reflect on this thought: How do I support their grasp of surface-level understanding, prompt deeper connections, and promote the transfer of their learning?

Drawing on cognitive load theory, offering students choices in how they learn, which resources to use, or how they show understanding helps manage cognitive load. This involves providing thoughtful personalization opportunities, not a complete lack of structure. For example, Jess's methods embed learning progression routines. By allowing learners to personalize their experience and choose resources or methods that match their strengths or preferences, we can reduce extraneous load from poorly presented information and inefficient pathways, freeing up working memory for essential processes (Clark, 2025).

STUDENT-FAMILY PARTNERSHIP REFLECTION

Igniting student motivation and reflection on success extends outside of the school setting. To foster an authentic partnership with students and families, share these questions with them to promote reflection on the student's learning journey and success.

- How is learning in school connected to personal interests, future goals, or what you want to do in life?
- How do you know when you are truly learning and making progress, not just completing assignments or getting grades?
- What experiences or resources help you feel motivated and challenged to think critically?

When it seems appropriate, have families and students share their reflections, completing the cycle of purpose.

The Big Ideas

In this chapter, we explored the significance of purpose in learning and how to cultivate it in educational environments. We established a vision for the learning journey by unlocking the essence of learning intentions and intentionally sharing purpose through three key strategies: planning, communicating, and sharing purpose. Purpose-based learning emphasizes effort, growth, and an innovative mindset, valuing progress and challenges over grades. This includes creating a learner profile based on classroom values and documenting the ideal student journey.

A clear vision, grounded in a shared understanding of learning's purpose, can guide all involved and foster resilience. Clarity can be established through intentional explanations, examples, and guided practice with self-assessment. Success criteria signal learners about their destination and provide a map for reaching it. Empowering students to own their learning is crucial in clarifying success. Effective classrooms help students find personal meaning in learning and connect to their future beyond the curriculum.

Let's Reflect

How can you collaboratively establish and convey a common vision for success and growth within our classroom, encompassing not only specific tasks but also the entire learning journey?

____

____

____

In what ways might you be more deliberate when integrating purposeful learning into lessons and activities?

____

____

____

What strategies will help you intentionally connect the learning materials and activities to students' interests, ambitions, and sense of purpose?

____

____

____

What steps could you take to ensure that students comprehend the indicators of successful learning, utilizing clear and diverse success criteria?

____

____

____

What's Next?

Coming up in Chapter 3, "Moving From Groups to Team Collaboration," we will investigate how to make the shift toward students developing collective student efficacy and working toward shared goals. Effective collaboration nurtures skills like active listening, empathy, leadership, and social influence—attributes crucial for achieving academic success and thriving in future careers. Chapter 3 emphasizes the significance of organized collaboration, support, and methods to foster an inclusive and effective teamwork culture.

CHAPTER 3

Move From Groups to Team Collaboration

Shondra slumped in her chair as her group began planning their science project. As usual, Liam and Sophia were taking charge, tossing out ideas and dividing tasks. Shondra had an idea too, but every time she opened her mouth to speak, someone else talked over her. Frustrated, she crossed her arms and stayed silent. If no one wanted to hear her thoughts, why bother? As the group continued discussing, Shondra pulled out her notebook and doodled, disengaging from the task. A few minutes later, their teacher, Mr. Reyes, walked over. "Shondra, what do you think about the project plan?" he asked. Shondra hesitated, then shrugged. "I don't know. No one listens anyway." Mr. Reyes nodded and turned to the group. "Let's pause for a second. I've noticed some ideas are getting lost. How can we make sure everyone's voice is heard?" Sophia looked at Shondra and said, "Oh . . . Shondra, did you have an idea?" Encouraged, Shondra sat up. "Yeah! What if we tested different soil types instead of just water levels? It might show different results." Liam grinned. "That's actually a cool idea!" With a little teacher guidance, Shondra began to see that her contributions mattered, and her group learned how to collaborate more inclusively.

WHY STUDENT COLLABORATION MATTERS

In today's rapidly evolving global economy, the ability to collaborate effectively has become a defining factor in workforce success. The nature of work is shifting dramatically due to technological advancements, globalization, and the increasing complexity of problem-solving across industries. According to the World Economic Forum's (2020) *Future of Jobs Report 2023*, employers rank teamwork and collaboration among the top skills needed for the future workforce. For example, automation and artificial intelligence are transforming job roles, reducing the demand for routine, individual tasks and amplifying the need for human centric skills such as communication, problem-solving, and adaptability—all of which are foundational to effective teamwork. The *Future of Jobs Report 2023* underscores this shift, revealing that social and emotional skills, including collaboration, will see a 24 percent increase in demand by 2030.

As a result, teaching students how to collaborate and function as part of a team is more critical than ever to their future careers. Educators play a vital role in preparing students to meet these workforce expectations by integrating teamwork-based learning experiences. Studies show that students who engage in collaborative learning demonstrate improved critical thinking, communication skills, and higher academic achievement. Research published in the *Journal of Educational Psychology* reports that cooperative learning enhances student engagement and long-term knowledge retention, skills that translate directly to workplace effectiveness (Johnson & Johnson, 2009). When students learn to navigate teamwork dynamics—such as resolving conflicts, sharing responsibilities, and leveraging diverse perspectives—they develop emotional intelligence and leadership capabilities. The Partnership for 21st Century Learning (P21) emphasizes that collaborative learning environments foster creativity and innovation, which are key drivers of economic growth and competitiveness in the global market.

In order to transform a classroom of individual learners into a classroom of interconnected thinkers where learning experiences are designed to nurture the attitudes and skills of collaboration, students must develop the ability to listen actively, communicate effectively, and engage in shared problem-solving that values diverse perspectives. In a collaborative learning environment, students work together in teams to achieve a common goal. "It is time to develop a culture of exchange and cooperation in our schools so that we can harness the power of collective intelligence to the benefit of learners and also to the benefit of teachers" (Hattie & Zierer, 2018, p. 33). The skills and behaviors required for effective teamwork extend beyond simply organizing students into groups for the sake of structuring differentiated learning activities. Rather, when students work together in teams, they develop collective student efficacy, believing that they can achieve their goals together. Underlying attitudes related to working with others—empathy, active listening, leadership, and social influence, for example—are fundamental to successful teams in the learning environment and transcend into crucial skills necessary for children's future careers (World Economic Forum, 2020).

To equip students with essential collaboration skills, schools and educators must actively integrate teamwork into curricula through project-based learning, group discussions, and real-world problem-solving exercises. Encouraging peer-to-peer collaboration, interdisciplinary projects, and digital collaboration tools will help students gain practical experience in teamwork, preparing them for the demands of modern workplaces. By cultivating the habit of collaboration and teamwork in the classroom, we ensure that students are not only prepared to enter the workforce but also equipped to thrive and lead in an interconnected, dynamic future (Figure 3.1).

FIGURE 3.1 • Characteristics of Collaboration

EFFECTIVE STUDENT COLLABORATION IS . . .	EFFECTIVE STUDENT COLLABORATION IS NOT . . .
• Designed with intentional structures and processes to foster students' skill development.	• Placing students in group work settings but only asking them to complete work individually.
• A routine practice utilized as an integral component of all instructional periods throughout a school day.	• Attained simply by organizing student seating arrangements into pairs or small groups.
• An opportunity to enable students to practice meaningful learning structures such as discussion, peer-to-peer teaching, and giving and receiving feedback.	• Attained without attending to social norms early and often to ensure healthy group behavior and interpersonal dynamics.

COLLABORATION CULTIVATES HEALTHY STUDENT LEARNING COMMUNITIES

The Collaborative for Social, Emotional, and Academic Learning (CASEL) offers a research-based framework within which relationship skills are identified as one of the five foundational areas of competence for development to support a healthy, fulfilling life. "This includes the capacities to communicate clearly, listen actively, cooperate, work collaboratively to problem solve and negotiate conflict constructively, navigate settings with differing social and cultural demands and opportunities, provide leadership, and seek or offer help when needed" (CASEL, n.d.). Nurturing students' development of the nuanced skills and mindsets surrounding collaborative behavior presents an opportunity to foster deeper empathy, active listening, adaptability, and a shared sense of responsibility, ultimately preparing them for meaningful teamwork in both academic and real-world learning communities.

CONNECTION

Developing collaboration skills will naturally present opportunities and challenges for learners also learning to embrace vulnerability. You'll explore this habit more specifically in Chapter 7.

Research also highlights how students learn more effectively in environments where they work together to achieve shared goals rather than in highly competitive settings (Hattie, 2023). Cooperative learning, the opposite of competitive learning, has a statistically significant effect of .59 (Hattie, 2023) on student learning and, when characterized by peer-to-peer teaching, active discussion, and problem-solving, leads to higher retention rates and critical thinking development for students. Yet, it is important to begin by recognizing that collaboration, cooperative learning, and becoming a learning team are skills and practices that require intentional design and direct instruction and development to yield the positive effects found in research. Throughout the rest of the chapter, you'll explore numerous approaches and activities designed to enable the development and cultivation of healthy collaboration and teamwork for your learners. First, however, let's examine why collaboration can present unique challenges based on students' developmental, social, and emotional needs.

Even as adults, you are likely familiar with the pitfalls of being placed into a collaborative environment without adequate time and effort invested into coming together in ways that are rewarding, meaningful, and psychologically safe for everyone involved. Collaboration can be challenging for students because of both their need for a sense of belonging and the hidden and explicit social norms that shape group behavior. Students, like all people, want to feel accepted and valued in a group. If they don't feel a sense of belonging, they may hesitate to participate, fear rejection, or struggle to assert their ideas. For example, a student who feels like an outsider may hold back to avoid saying something "wrong." Similarly, if a group has an established dynamic where certain voices dominate, quieter students may struggle to contribute. A lack of psychological safety can make students afraid of making mistakes, which stifles creativity and risk-taking.

Social norms, both unspoken (hidden) and clearly stated (explicit), also influence how students interact in groups. These norms can either support or hinder collaboration. For example, students may subconsciously follow patterns from past experiences, such as letting high-status peers lead or assuming certain roles based on gender, race, or perceived ability. Some norms are explicit and may even be designed by the teacher or members of the class. These classroom structures may impose clear rules about participation, turn-taking, or leadership, but if students don't understand or agree with them, they may disengage. When students are aware of social dynamics and feel a genuine sense of belonging, they are more likely to collaborate effectively. However, when norms exclude or silence certain voices, or when students don't feel accepted, collaboration becomes difficult.

FROM THE LENS OF A STUDENT

Mark Grapples With Social Dynamics

The group sat in a circle in the library, laptops open, brainstorming ideas for their history project. Ava scrolled through a document, barely looking up. "We should focus on how social media shapes political opinions," she said, and the others nodded in agreement. Mark hesitated before speaking. "What about misinformation during historical events? Like how propaganda influenced World War II?" Ava smirked. "That's kind of off topic." Beside her, Lila giggled. "Yeah, Mark, we're talking about now, not ancient history." Emma leaned in. "Do you even use social media? This project is about things people actually care about." Mark's face turned red. He opened his mouth, then closed it again, his fingers tightening around his notebook. The last time he pushed back, they rolled their eyes and exchanged looks like he wasn't worth listening to. Across the table, Jordan glanced at Mark, then back at his screen. He didn't agree with the girls, but speaking up meant risking their ridicule too. So, he kept quiet, letting the conversation move on without him.

Consider each student's experiences in the group activity described in the From the Lens of a Student box and how they may reflect group dynamics you have observed in your classroom. As you prepare to explore specific strategies for addressing some typical pitfalls of collaboration, use the reflection chart shown in the Pause and Reflect box to journal the social dynamics you believe may be present in this particular group as well as what strategies you currently feel comfortable employing to mitigate the impact of negative social norms on your students' ability to collaborate effectively.

Pause and Reflect

What do you notice about the nonverbal behavior of each of the different students and how it affects the other members of the group?	
What do you wonder about the structure of the learning activity and the impact of this structure on the group dynamics?	
What strategies might you suggest a teacher employ in order to enhance the ability of these students to collaborate more effectively?	

ADDRESSING COMMON COLLABORATION CHALLENGES

When students are asked to engage in a group for the purpose of any sort of learning experience, it is important to attend to the fundamental needs of each group member in order for them to experience a sense of belonging in the group. This is a crucial step to enable learning behaviors to occur. Dysfunctional group dynamics often stem from a lack of belonging. Here are some strategies that can help address common group collaboration challenges.

STRATEGY 1: CONSTRUCTIVE AND DESTRUCTIVE GROUP BEHAVIORS PROTOCOL

The Constructive and Destructive Group Behaviors Protocol is a structured approach to identifying, understanding, and managing behaviors that either enhance or hinder collaboration in group settings. This protocol is often used to foster effective teamwork, communication, and problem-solving. To begin, let's examine the distinctions between different types of behavior that are either constructive (enhance collaboration and productivity) or destructive (undermine collaboration and productivity) in group learning environments, as shown in Figure 3.2.

FIGURE 3.2 • Constructive vs. Destructive Group Behaviors

CONSTRUCTIVE BEHAVIORS **These behaviors help groups work efficiently, maintain positive relationships, and achieve their goals.**	**DESTRUCTIVE BEHAVIORS** **These behaviors disrupt teamwork, create conflict, or hinder progress.**
Active Listening: Members listen attentively, make eye contact, and respond thoughtfully.	**Dominating the Discussion:** One or more members control the conversation, limiting input from others.
Encouraging Participation: Group members invite others to contribute and ensure all voices are heard.	**Ignoring or Dismissing Ideas:** Contributions from some members are overlooked or undervalued.
Respectful Disagreement: Differences in opinion are welcomed and discussed constructively.	**Negative Attitudes and Complaining:** Constant negativity lowers morale and makes collaboration difficult.
Clarifying and Summarizing: Participants restate key points to ensure shared understanding.	**Blaming and Defensiveness:** Instead of focusing on solutions, group members assign blame or refuse to accept constructive criticism.
Equal Contribution: Workload is distributed fairly, and everyone plays an active role.	**Social Loafing (Free Riding)**: Some members contribute little or avoid responsibility.
Staying Solution Focused: The group works toward solving problems rather than assigning blame.	**Side Conversations and Distractions:** Off-topic discussions reduce focus and derail progress.
Adaptability and Open-Mindedness: Members remain flexible and willing to adjust their thinking.	**Groupthink:** Members conform to the majority opinion rather than critically evaluating ideas.
Timely and Constructive Feedback: Feedback is specific, helpful, and aimed at improving ideas rather than criticizing individuals.	**Untimely and Unhelpful Feedback:** Feedback is vague, overly critical, or delayed, often targeting individuals rather than ideas and hindering group progress.

IMPLEMENTING THE PROTOCOL IN THE CLASSROOM

To help students recognize and manage these constructive and destructive group behaviors, using the following steps provides an entry point for intentional application and reflection:

1. **Set Clear Group Norms:** At the start of a group activity, discuss what effective collaboration looks like. Provide a list of constructive and destructive behaviors and ask students to reflect on past experiences. Have each group create their own norms (e.g., "We will listen before responding" or "We will share responsibility fairly").
2. **Assign Group Roles to Promote Constructive Behaviors:** To balance participation, assign roles such as the following:
   - Facilitator: Ensures all voices are heard
   - Timekeeper: Keeps the group on track
   - Encourager: Ensures a positive and respectful atmosphere
   - Alternate Perspective: Challenges ideas to deepen discussion
3. **Monitor and Provide Feedback:** Observe student interactions and take note of both productive and unproductive behaviors. Use a "pause and reflect" moment mid activity to ask "What's working well?" and "What needs to improve?" As you guide students in their reflection, use sentence starters to support open-ended dialogue, such as "I wonder if . . ." or "What patterns do you see?"
4. **End With Reflection and Self-Assessment:** Have students complete a group behavior reflection responding to questions such as the following:
   - "What constructive behaviors helped us succeed?"
   - "Did we experience any destructive behaviors? How did we handle them?"
   - "What will we improve for next time?"

Use peer evaluations to provide anonymous feedback on group dynamics.

STRATEGY 2: CREATING A SAFE SPACE FOR INQUIRY

Collaboration experts Bruce Wellman and Laura Lipton (2024) provide a structured approach for adult professional learning communities (PLCs) to analyze information collaboratively, promote critical thinking, and make informed decisions. The same principles can be applied to student learning communities (SLCs) with the goal of creating a safe space for inquiry. As described throughout the chapter thus far, we know that effective collaboration begins with a trusting, nonjudgmental environment where participants feel comfortable exploring new ideas and questions without fear of being wrong. Group work often involves pursuits wherein students will be asked to examine new information, organize different perspectives approaches from across the group, and synthesize their understanding of the ideas or concepts to share with others. Building upon the constructive behavior activity from strategy 1, teach students the skill of collaborative inquiry using a protocol that requires participants to suspend judgment and listen to understand rather than respond. Here are three phases for analyzing information (Wellman & Lipton, 2024:

Phase 1—Activate and Engage Preconceptions and Prior Knowledge: When tackling a group project, encourage brainstorming and mind mapping before diving into detailed research or problem-solving. Require students to surface their initial thoughts and assumptions by posing these questions:

- "What do we already know about this topic?"
- "What do we think will be the biggest challenges?"

The most productive collaborations focus on asking better questions, not just finding answers. Encourage students to use higher-order questioning techniques (e.g., "How might this problem be approached differently?"). Have groups generate their own questions before receiving direct instruction. Model and support curiosity and adaptability by allowing students to refine their approaches as they collaborate.

Phase 2—Explore, Discover, and Analyze Without Bias: As groups of students engage in examining new concepts, pieces of data or evidence, or subject-area content, for example, they may be at risk for asserting specific conclusions or judgments based on unconscious bias or personal experience. These behaviors are natural but can also serve to diminish other group members' curiosity if ideas become too quickly adopted. Encourage students to explore data objectively, looking for patterns, contradictions, and surprises before jumping to conclusions with some of the following techniques:

- In a science experiment, have students analyze results using neutral language (e.g., "The data show . . ." rather than "We were right/wrong").

- In a literature discussion, students can examine character development or themes by collecting textual evidence before forming interpretations.
- Use graphic organizers (e.g., T-charts, Venn diagrams) to help students visually analyze and compare information.

Phase 3—Organize, Integrate, Draw Conclusions, and Take Action: Group learning experiences commonly lead to opportunities for students to collaboratively synthesize their new understandings and share them with the broader learning community. While modes of communication may vary depending on the learning intentions, consider the opportunity to highlight the connection between the collaboration skills they practiced and their ongoing development of constructive group behaviors. Encourage students to connect their findings to real-world applications (e.g., "How does this relate to issues in our community?").

Use reflection prompts:

- "What did we learn from this process?"
- "How did our initial thoughts change?"
- "What do we still need to investigate?"

By incorporating these strategies, classroom collaboration becomes more structured, meaningful, and reflective, helping students develop critical thinking and teamwork skills—all essential for future learning and careers.

FROM THE LENS OF A TEACHER

Mr. Ramirez's Approach to Cultivating Collaboration

During a recent art class, Mr. Ramirez's fourth graders were working on a mural project focused on community. At first, he was excited to see their enthusiasm—paint flying, ideas bouncing. But it quickly became clear that "working together" meant something different to each of them. Some students dominated decisions, others stood back silently, and small disagreements turned into big frustrations. He overheard Jordan snap at Maya for "messing up his idea," while two others argued over who got to choose the colors. He paused the class. They sat in a circle, brushes down, and Mr. Ramirez asked them to reflect: What makes teamwork feel good? What makes it hard? Their answers surprised Mr. Ramirez. "It's hard when no one listens," one student shared. Another added, "I don't want to argue, but I also want my ideas in the mural." That moment became a turning point. Together, they co-created a list of "Collaboration Norms"—things like listening first, offering kind feedback, and agreeing on a shared vision before starting. Now, every art class begins with a quick check-in using those norms. And while it's still messy sometimes, Mr. Ramirez can see them learning what it means to create together and not just beside one another.

STRATEGY 3: COLLABORATION TO DEVELOP STUDENT COLLECTIVE EFFICACY

Just like adults, and like the students in Mr. Ramirez's classroom, students experience varying degrees of self-efficacy (described in Chapter 1 where you examined the relationship between students' belief systems and their confidence in being able to learn, for example). Collective efficacy is equally important as self-efficacy and enables groups of learners in a community to mutually support one another's capacity to achieve rigorous learning tasks. The behaviors and attitudes described in Figure 3.3, for example, reflect a blend of "I" skills and "we" skills that support development of collective efficacy. When teaching students these types of skills, consider first conducting an inventory of student understanding to illuminate opportunities for new learning.

Figure 3.3 can be used to explore prior knowledge and prepare to activate new learning for your students.

Save this reflection chart for review as you delve more deeply into the habits presented in the forthcoming chapters! For example, research shows that peer collaboration in feedback is shown to have a significant effect on student learning (0.75) (Hattie, 2023). Students who work together to review, discuss, and refine their understanding see substantial learning gains, and Chapter 5, "Navigate the Feedback Process," will support you and your students in a deep exploration of this specific skill to foster collective efficacy and effective collaboration! Classroom discussion is also a highly impactful practice (effect size 0.82) that engages many of the "I" and "we" skills described in Figure 3.3. Chapter 7, "Embrace Vulnerability," offers explicit opportunities for teaching the routines and structures that enable your students to engage effectively in classroom discussion.

FIGURE 3.3 ● Student Inventory: Prior Knowledge of Constructive Group Behavior

CONSTRUCTIVE GROUP BEHAVIOR	WHAT DOES THIS LOOK AND SOUND LIKE AS AN "I" SKILL (E.G., WHEN I DISPLAY THIS BEHAVIOR)	WHAT DOES IT FEEL LIKE FOR ME WHEN OTHER GROUP MEMBERS DISPLAY THIS AS A "WE" SKILL
Active Listening: Members listen attentively, make eye contact, and respond thoughtfully.		
Encouraging Participation: Group members invite others to contribute and ensure all voices are heard.		
Respectfully Disagreeing: Differences in opinion are welcomed and discussed constructively.		
Clarifying and Summarizing: Participants restate key points to ensure shared understanding.		
Staying Solution Focused: The group works toward solving problems rather than assigning blame.		
Contributing Equally: Workload is distributed fairly, and everyone plays an active role.		
Displaying Adaptability and Open-Mindedness: Members remain flexible and willing to adjust their thinking.		
Giving Timely and Constructive Feedback: Feedback is specific, helpful, and aimed at improving ideas rather than criticizing individuals.		

Pause and Reflect

Building upon your learning from Chapters 1 and 2 as well as the trends you notice in your students' responses to the chart in Figure 3.3, now complete the reflection chart below for your own planning as you identify specific areas of the Constructive Group Behaviors where your students may need explicit instruction for further development.

Specific "I" skills that my students demonstrate solid understanding are:	
Specific "we" skills that my students demonstrate solid understanding are:	
I noticed that my students need to develop their skills in the following "we" skill areas:	

STUDENT LEARNING TEAMS CULTIVATE RESILIENCE TOGETHER

As you learned in the first chapters of this book, according to the science of positive psychology, resilience is defined as the ability to adapt and thrive in the face of adversity, challenges, and stress. It is not merely about "bouncing back" from difficulties but also about growing stronger and developing greater emotional and psychological flexibility. Educators can teach students to cultivate personal resilience through a combination of developing internal strengths—such as optimism, self-efficacy, and emotional regulation—and building external support systems, including healthy relationships and collaborative environments. Students build resilience when they engage in collaborative learning experiences that require critical thinking, adaptability, and mutual support. Experiencing collaboration through learning teams enables students to foster resilience by teaching them how to navigate challenges, manage differing perspectives, and persist through difficulties. Consider the skills shown in Figure 3.4 that are required for collaboration and how they support students' individual resilience.

FIGURE 3.4 • Collaboration Skills That Build Resilience

COLLABORATION SKILL	CONNECTION BETWEEN SKILLS AND RESILIENCE
Overcoming Setbacks Together	When students work on a complex project, they often encounter challenges, such as conflicting viewpoints, incomplete information, or unforeseen obstacles. By developing strategies to navigate these challenges—such as active listening, compromise, and problem-solving—they build resilience both individually and as a team.
Strengthening Arguments With Research	When students learn to support their ideas with credible sources, they develop intellectual resilience. Instead of being discouraged when their initial ideas are challenged, they learn to refine their thinking through evidence. This process encourages curiosity and the ability to adapt one's viewpoint in light of new information.
Building a Supportive Team Culture	Group resilience is strengthened when students learn to encourage each other, give constructive feedback, and distribute responsibilities equitably. When every member feels valued and supported, they are more likely to take risks, share ideas, and stay engaged even when the project becomes difficult.
Developing Confidence in Problem-Solving	Through collaborative research and discussion, students gain confidence in their ability to contribute meaningfully. This personal resilience transfers to future learning experiences, equipping them to handle academic and real-world challenges with persistence and adaptability.

By engaging in structured group learning activities that emphasize teamwork, students learn that resilience is not just about individual perseverance—it is also about relying on and supporting others to achieve shared success. As students experience collaborative learning teams and develop and refine their skills, they may be rewarded with a strong, healthy support network. Resilience is further nurtured when individuals are surrounded with positive relationships from which they may receive encouragement, reassurance, and perspective. When sharing the collective goal of solving a problem with a group, students will be required to listen to diverse perspectives and adapt their approaches based on group input, thus developing their ability to navigate uncertainty and change effectively. Ultimately, collaboration teaches students that resilience is not just an individual trait but also a skill that can be strengthened through social connections and shared experiences.

STUDENT-FAMILY PARTNERSHIP REFLECTION

To deepen the power of the strategies you learned in this chapter, support students' development of collaboration skills by creating intentional opportunities for reflection and dialogue at home. With these guiding questions, families can reinforce the habits and mindsets students are practicing in the classroom.

1. Can you share a time when you worked with others to solve a problem? What made the teamwork successful or challenging?
2. When you're working with a group of friends or classmates, how do you make sure everyone's ideas are heard and valued?
3. How do you feel when you help someone in a group and when others help you? Why do you think that matters?

Just as you explored in earlier chapters, consider inviting families to share their reflection conversations, further fostering a collaborative school community.

The Big Ideas

In Chapters 1 and 2, you examined the transformative power of clarifying students' "why."

When students understand their purpose in education, they become more engaged, motivated, and invested in their growth. By learning to guide students to define their "why," you are empowered to foster deeper connections to learning and set the stage for them to take ownership of their academic and personal goals. This chapter explored the shift where students develop collective efficacy and work toward shared goals. Effective teamwork fosters critical skills such as active listening, empathy, leadership, and social influence—qualities essential for both academic success and future careers. This chapter also highlighted the importance of structured collaboration, teacher guidance, and strategies to cultivate a culture of inclusivity and productive teamwork.

Let's Reflect

Reflect on a recent group activity you applied in your classroom. Using what you have learned in this chapter, how could you shift the experience toward true team collaboration, ensuring every student feels valued and heard?

____

____

____

What common challenges do your students face when working in teams (e.g., social norms, belonging, group dynamics)? How might implementing constructive group behaviors and group norms improve their teamwork skills?

____

____

____

Considering the increasing importance of teamwork in the contemporary workforce, what strategies from this chapter might you prioritize integrating into your teaching to develop students' collaboration, leadership, and problem-solving skills for long-term success?

____

____

____

What's Next?

Looking ahead to Chapter 4, about student goal-setting, you'll apply concepts and strategies around student efficacy and beliefs toward guiding learners to set meaningful and achievable academic and personal goals. You'll unpack strategies for helping students develop a growth mindset, track progress effectively, and take ownership of their learning through structured goal-setting frameworks. By building on the habits of clarifying student success and effective collaboration, these goal-setting strategies will set the stage for teaching students to navigate the feedback process, the topic of Chapter 5!

CHAPTER 4

Empower Learners Through Goal-Setting

In a lively classroom bustling with eager learners, Josefina, a high school sophomore struggling to find motivation and academic direction, embarked on a transformative journey. With the support of her dedicated teacher, Mr. Wheeler, Josefina began setting personalized learning goals that resonated with her own aspirations and ambitions. Through their meaningful discussions and targeted guidance, Josefina gained a sense of ownership over her education and developed a clear vision for her future academic success. With newfound agency and purpose, she experienced a significant shift in her academic journey. Driven by her defined learning objectives, Josefina felt a renewed sense of motivation and determination, inspiring her to strive for excellence in her studies. As she worked toward her goals, she not only elevated her academic performance but also cultivated a stronger sense of self-confidence and resilience. Witnessing Josefina's remarkable growth and achievements, Mr. Wheeler recognized the profound impact of empowering students to take charge of their learning paths. This empowering approach not only unlocked Josefina's full potential but also showcased the transformative influence of personalized goal-setting on student engagement, growth, and overall academic success.

WHY GOAL-SETTING WITH STUDENTS MATTERS

Research unequivocally highlights the pivotal role of student agency in shaping goal-setting and academic achievement. Student agency is the transformative ability of learners to take proactive control of their educational journey, fostering a sense of ownership, autonomy, and purpose in their pursuit of knowledge and personal growth. As educators, we understand the profound impact of empowering students to take the reins of their learning journey and actively shape their educational path. This deliberate cultivation of autonomy and control not only nurtures the ability to establish purposeful and attainable goals but also serves as a powerful catalyst for heightened motivation, self-regulation, and overall engagement in the realm of education. When students use agency to actively engage in goal-setting, they demonstrate the transformative potential of fostering a dynamic and participatory learning environment—one that aligns with our mission as educators and guides us in how we craft strategies, systems, and supports for their success.

As Chase Nordengren stated (2022),

> The heart of an effective goal-setting process lies in the students themselves. Whether we choose to acknowledge it or not, students are responsible for when, where, and how they will learn. While a teacher can never force students to apply themselves to the task of learning, there are many tools at the teacher's disposal to motivate and engage students in the hard work of learning. (p. 29)

Furthermore, in our first book, *Habits of Resilient Educators* (Prendergast & Lee, 2024), we identified the powerful move goal-setting has on educators and students:

> When teachers set up systems that target personalized learning goals for students, this positively impacts the teacher–student relationship and academic growth and achievement of each learner. Students should receive support with their personalized learning goals through small groups or one-on-one mini sessions to help each student meet their own academic or behavioral goals. Creating systems or "habits" in the classroom to both set and monitor goals can be done with students instead of for students. (p. 92)

In addition, creating a classroom environment that emphasizes mastery goals is crucial for fostering student success. Mastery goals means students are focusing on achieving a deep understanding of concepts and skills (Murayama & Elliot, 2009). Encouraging students to focus on setting mastery-oriented goals helps them build resilience, nurture a growth mindset, and stay motivated from within. This approach not only guides students toward deeper understanding and skill mastery but also instills a strong sense of purpose in their educational journey. Embracing mastery-oriented goal-setting ensures that every student has the opportunity to thrive and excel, paving the way for continuous improvement and academic achievement in the classroom.

As seasoned educators, we understand the impact goal-setting has on student outcomes and that it is not a one-size-fits-all approach. Just like any instructional method or intervention, the effectiveness of student goal-setting pivots on the careful design and implementation of our strategies. It is crucial to recognize that setting goals in isolation may not automatically yield positive results for our students. The key lies in our ability to thoughtfully craft and execute personalized goal-setting practices that resonate with each learner's unique needs and aspirations (see Figure 4.1). By tailoring our approach to encompass individualized support and targeted guidance, we can harness the true potential of goal-setting to drive student efficacy, growth, and achievement. Let us leverage our expertise and empathy to design goal-setting frameworks that nurture student development and foster a culture of achievement in our educational settings.

FIGURE 4.1 ● Characteristics of Goal-Setting

EFFECTIVE GOAL-SETTING IS . . .	EFFECTIVE GOAL-SETTING IS NOT . . .
• Purposeful, specific, clearly defined, measurable, and aligned with learning objectives.	• Arbitrary, vague, or lacking specificity and relevance, thus leading to confusion and lack of motivation.
• Mastery-driven and focused on achieving a deep understanding of concepts and skills.	• Excessively performance-driven, which tends to encourage seeking external validation and comparing oneself to others.
• An empowering practice that encourages students to take ownership of their learning.	• Imposed on students without their input, potentially hindering motivation and engagement.
• Motivation for students, inspiring them to strive for success and develop a growth mindset.	• Demoralizing: Unrealistic or unattainable goals can demotivate students and impede progress.
• An ongoing process that students engage in over and over as part of their normal learning process.	• A "one-off" experience for students that is seen as something done once and never revisited or revised.

FROM THE LENS OF A TEACHER

Mrs. Thompson's Journey Through Celebrations and Challenges in Goal-Setting

In her vibrant elementary classroom, Mrs. Thompson, a dedicated and experienced teacher, faced a familiar challenge: motivating a diverse group of young learners. Seeking a fresh approach, she introduced goal-setting as a tool to boost engagement and inspire ownership of learning. At first, the transition wasn't easy. Her students, still developing their self-awareness, struggled to articulate goals in a structured way. Recognizing this, Mrs. Thompson took intentional steps to model the process. She led class discussions about setting small, meaningful goals connected to personal interests, gradually building her students' understanding. With patience and guidance, she created a routine that gave students the confidence to express their dreams and track their progress. Over time, Mrs. Thompson observed a powerful shift—students who were once hesitant began articulating their aspirations with clarity and purpose. Goal-setting transformed from a foreign concept into an empowering routine. Her classroom blossomed into a space where learners were motivated, focused, and excited to grow. Through intentional modeling, scaffolding, and persistence, Mrs. Thompson cultivated a culture of ambition and self-direction. She began to see firsthand how goal-setting—when implemented with care and adaptability—could unlock her students' potential and foster a lifelong love for learning.

ROUTINES AND PROCEDURES THAT SUPPORT THE HABIT OF GOAL-SETTING

As a result of today's highly distracted and digital culture, procedures and routines are crucial when it comes to setting, monitoring, and achieving academic goals for all students. One common misconception in the American education system is that students and teachers can effectively and efficiently multitask while navigating multiple technology platforms within a very short amount of time. However, research suggests that there is a strong correlation between multitasking and decreased productivity (American Psychological Association, 2020). Furthermore, the ability for students to focus on one task is decreasing at alarming rates (Gaddi, 2025). The average attention span of the human, according to a study from Microsoft Corporation, is reported to be just 8 seconds, signaling the impact of an increasingly digitized lifestyle (McSpadden, 2015). When considering the most common distractions hindering students from achieving their academic goals, a plethora of factors comes into play. Many students are faced with challenges such as digital media overload, multitasking, and lack of effective time management skills. In a digital age where students are constantly bombarded by notifications, emails, and social media updates, maintaining focus on academic tasks becomes increasingly challenging. Furthermore, attempting to multitask, a habit often perceived as a skill by students, can actually lead to decreased productivity and hindered goal attainment. Addressing these distractions and fostering a learning environment that encourages mindfulness, single-tasking, and prioritization is crucial in supporting students to overcome these common barriers and succeed academically.

Furthermore, working with students to set goals—both collectively and individually—actively builds the habit of goal-setting and reinforces it as a meaningful practice. Distraction can be the enemy to achieving goals and helping students get into the practice of identifying what distracts and motivates them. Identifying distractions and motivations will help them become more resilient with the habit of goal-setting.

In order to guide students toward optimizing their personalized learning goals, it is essential for students to identify factors that both motivate and distract them. By recognizing these elements, students can proactively enhance their learning experiences and navigate challenges effectively. Prioritizing motivating factors while mitigating distractions is key to fostering a conducive environment for academic success in education today. The list in Figure 4.2 is a starting place, and students should be invited to add to the list and come up with what uniquely impacts their learning.

FIGURE 4.2 ● Motivators and Distractors That Impact Progress Toward Learning Goals

MOTIVATORS	DISTRACTORS
• Effective goal-setting and tracking progress • Collaboration and peer support • Opportunities for choice and autonomy • Personalized learning paths • Sense of achievement and progress	• Technology notifications: social media, texts, emails • Overwhelm from high workload or expectations • Lack of clear direction or guidance • Burnout or stress from multitasking • Fear of failure or making mistakes

In addition, when setting up procedures and routines for goal-setting, it is vital to employ effective tools that provide a clear framework for students to reflect on their progress toward their goals. The Goal-Setting Reflective Rubric shown in Figure 4.3 offers a structured approach that allows students to self-assess their level of mastery and seek appropriate support when needed. The rubric's progressive scale, from acknowledging the need for reteaching to reaching mastery levels, empowers students to take ownership of their learning journey and fosters a growth mindset. By utilizing this rubric, educators can guide students in assessing their progress objectively and identifying the necessary strategies for continuous improvement, thereby promoting a culture of self-awareness and accountability in pursuit of their learning goals.

FIGURE 4.3 • Goal-Setting Reflective Rubric

Goal:	**1**	**2**	**3**	**4**
	I haven't master this goal yet. I need to be shown again how to learn this goal.	I can do some of this, but I need help from: __________ name	I can do this independently. I understand it and just need to keep purposefully practicing.	I am an expert at this and have mastered this goal. I can help others to learn it.

Adapted from Nordengren (2022, p. 18).

Also, teachers must establish a structured daily student schedule for focused meetings on personalized learning goals. Similar to appointments with a dentist or doctor, these scheduled interactions serve as vital touchpoints for student progress and success. Just as a patient arrives prepared for a medical appointment, students too must come ready for these sessions, equipped with their reflections, questions, and goals, mirroring the educator's commitment to guide and support their academic journey with precision and purpose. This proactive approach not only enhances student accountability but also underscores the educator's dedication to fostering a collaborative and goal-oriented learning environment that achieves tangible results. These routines must not just appear in a classroom but must be discussed and modeled regularly for students to have the conditions of success needed for goal-setting.

Pause and Reflect

How can you design and model classroom routines that help students minimize distractions and strengthen their ability to focus on setting and achieving meaningful goals?

In what ways might you use tools like reflective rubrics and scheduled goal-setting meetings to build students' ownership, accountability, and resilience in their learning process?'

Chappuis and Stiggins (2020) identify six different types of conferences that can be used to discuss students' goals. It is important to know the focus of a collaborative goal-setting conference so that both the student and the educator are effective and efficient with the precious time they have together to work on the mastery of a goal.

Chappuis and Stiggins's (2020) six types of conferences around goals are the following:

1. **Feedback conferences** focus on reviewing learning artifacts and identifying next steps toward a learning target.
2. **Goal-setting conferences** focus on considering where the student is now and setting a new goal.
3. **Progress conferences** focus on examining where the student is relative to their goal.
4. **Achievement-status conferences** focus on sharing results from an assessment.

5. **Showcase conferences** focus on allowing the student to demonstrate their mastery of content.
6. **Intervention conferences** focus on an area of academic concern, allowing participants to make plans to remedy that concern.

The chart in Figure 4.4 provides a clear framework for a teacher to schedule daily one-on-one sessions with each student, enabling focused attention and personalized goal-setting discussions. It allows for easy tracking of individual interactions and ensures that each student receives consistent support and guidance in line with their learning objectives. The Goal-Setting Weekly Agenda (Figure 4.4) can also be a terrific support during the one-on-one goal-setting session.

FIGURE 4.4 ● Sample Goal-Setting Weekly Agenda

DAY	STUDENT 1	STUDENT 2	STUDENT 3
Monday	Name: Type of Conference: Goal: Action Steps:	Name: Type of Conference: Goal: Action Steps:	Name: Type of Conference: Goal: Action Steps:
Tuesday	Name: Type of Conference: Goal: Action Steps:	Name: Type of Conference: Goal: Action Steps:	Name: Type of Conference: Goal: Next Steps:
Wednesday	Name: Type of Conference: Goal: Action Steps:	Name: Type of Conference: Goal: Action Steps:	Name: Type of Conference: Goal: Action Steps:

DAY	STUDENT 1	STUDENT 2	STUDENT 3
Thursday	Name: Type of Conference: Goal: Action Steps:	Name: Type of Conference: Goal: Action Steps:	Name: Type of Conference: Goal: Action Steps:
Friday	Name: Type of Conference: Goal: Action Steps:	Name: Type of Conference: Goal: Action Steps:	Name: Type of Conference: Goal: Action Steps:

GOAL-SETTING WITHIN THE FORMATIVE ASSESSMENT CYCLE

The Formative Assessment Cycle, shown in Figure 4.5, plays a pivotal role in shaping goal-setting and monitoring practices. By posing the fundamental questions of "Where is the learner going?" and "Where is the learner now?" this cycle creates a roadmap for targeted educational growth. Within this cycle, the empowered learning team—comprised of the individual learner, peers, and educators—collaborates to facilitate progress. With its four key components—clarifying learning, activating learners, eliciting and analyzing evidence, and providing actionable feedback—this cycle not only guides learners in understanding their learning objectives but also empowers them to take ownership of their educational journey by engaging with peers and educators. Ultimately, the Formative Assessment Cycle not only informs goal-setting but also ensures that monitoring is grounded in evidence-based insights, fostering a culture of continuous improvement and personalized learning strategies.

FIGURE 4.5 ● Formative Assessment Cycle

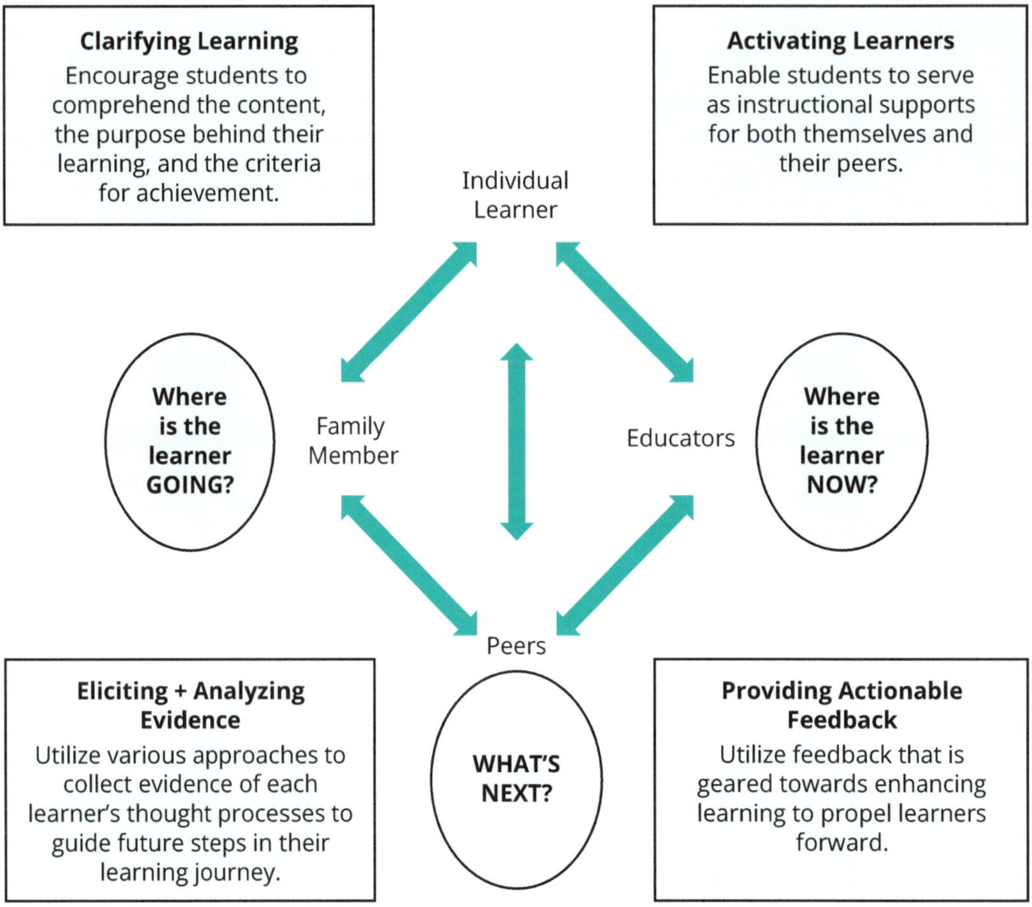

GUIDING THE WAY: MASTERFULLY BALANCING FEEDBACK, ASSESSMENT, AND GOAL ANALYSIS

Setting up the optimal conditions for delivering feedback on students' personalized learning goals requires a strategic approach that blends empathy, structure, and clarity.

Educators must first establish a supportive and inclusive classroom culture where students feel safe to set and work toward their individual objectives. By fostering an environment of trust and respect, educators create a foundation for open communication and constructive feedback exchanges. This collaborative approach not only increases student engagement and ownership but also sets the stage for personalized feedback that resonates with each learner.

CONNECTION

In Chapter 5, we will dive more deeply into helping students navigate the feedback process.

In addition to cultivating a nurturing classroom atmosphere, educators must implement systems and routines that facilitate regular feedback loops tailored to students' personalized learning goals. Structured checkpoints, such as daily reflections, goal-setting conferences, or progress tracking sessions, provide opportunities for educators to monitor student growth closely and intervene when necessary. Often educators are rumbling with how to manage time constraints, goal-setting conferences, daily reflections, and progress tracking. Unfortunately, these are some of the first things to get cut from the schedule. However, the truth is that the fortune is in the follow-up when it comes to providing feedback to students' learning goals and is something that needs to be treated with urgency. Also, clear communication channels and well-defined expectations help streamline the feedback process, making it more effective and actionable for both students and teachers. By establishing consistent feedback procedures and routines that are transparent, personalized, time bound and actionable, educators are modeling the importance of setting, monitoring, and celebrating student learning and behavioral goals.

FROM THE LENS OF A STUDENT

Alex's Self-Efficacy Restored Through Goal-Setting

Midway through the school year at Clearwater Middle School, Alex, a brand new sophomore at the school, felt the weight of his reading challenges. Words blurred, comprehension slipped away, and frustration grew each time he opened a book. His confidence faltered, and he began to wonder if reading would ever feel enjoyable.

When Ms. Daniels noticed his struggle, she approached Alex with quiet understanding. She suggested they work together to build his reading skills, not through pressure but with a plan tailored just for him. They set achievable goals—specific, measurable, and tied to his personal interests and long-term dreams. For the first time, Alex felt a sense of direction and purpose in his reading. Ms. Daniels introduced a reading log, encouraging Alex to track each session and reflect on his progress. Initially skeptical, Alex soon noticed how the log revealed his growth over time. Each completed entry became proof that he was improving, gradually restoring his motivation and sense of ownership over his learning. What made the biggest difference was how well Ms. Daniels understood his passions. Acting like a "book whisperer," she curated a reading list that connected his academic needs with his love for sports and adventure. These books spoke to him, bridging his challenges and his interests. Slowly, Alex began picking up books on his own—not as an assignment, but as an invitation to worlds he wanted to explore.

INSPECTING WHAT WE EXPECT

Offering feedback is a powerful move that supports and celebrates student progress in their learning and behavioral objectives. To truly maximize the impact of feedback, it is essential to provide specific and detailed insights related to the task at hand, encouraging students to engage in thoughtful analysis. For instance, in striving to enhance academic vocabulary, it is imperative to prompt students to reflect on their own advancements alongside teacher-provided feedback. By pausing after independent reading sessions to discuss the academic vocabulary goal and offering observations like, "I noticed you wrote down some academic vocabulary and then wrote impressive synonyms next to those vocabulary words to help you better understand the text," students not only receive targeted feedback but also engage in collaborative recognition of incremental achievements.

> When working with individual students during their one-on-one mini goal-setting conferences, it is essential to provide feedback on the progression of learning within the personalized learning goal. For example, if a student is working on using context clues from the text to support their vocabulary development, the teacher and student can look up the words that the student documented in their goal notebook and determine if/which context clues they are using. The teacher can help the student to analyze their work and provide specific feedback on their goal. (Prendergast & Lee, 2024, p. 102)

Again, this feedback should be noticeably clear and more detailed than "You did a great job." Providing clear feedback around vocabulary may sound like, "You are using the description and definition context clues effectively. Next, we will need to work on using inferences to determine unknown words." Providing specific feedback to a student on their goal is invaluable.

The chart in Figure 4.6 can be used to guide students in setting goals, determining how the students want to receive feedback, and reflecting and celebrating when the goal is accomplished. It is crucial to regularly monitor a student's progress toward their learning goal and offer timely, supportive feedback as they navigate the challenges involved in reaching it. Finally, when we reflect on and celebrate small milestones in learning goals, we help students recognize how goal-setting and feedback have strengthened their resilience.

FIGURE 4.6 ● Sample Goal-Setting Graphic Organizer

Step 1: Select a Goal

My goal is:

Why do I want to achieve this goal?

Date to achieve this goal by (Is this a weekly or monthly goal?):

What barriers do I think I might encounter while working on this goal and why?	What solutions can I try when I get stuck?

Resources I need to achieve this goal
1.
2.
3.

(Continued)

(Continued)

Step 2: Feedback

Who will provide feedback while working on this goal? (Circle one or two)

Peer | Family member | Teacher | Coach | Self-assessment

How I best receive feedback: (Circle one or two)

Written | Rubrics and scores | Verbal one on one | Verbal in a small group | AI

Step 3: Reflection

What was easy while working on this goal?

What was hard while working on this goal?

Notes from my experience learning this goal:

Step 4: Celebrate the Small Milestones

How do I like to celebrate achieving my learning goals? (Circle one or two)

- Verbally: Shout-out from teacher publically
- Verbally: Shout-out from teacher one on one
- Written: A note from a teacher to me
- Written: An email or note to tell my family
- Earn points toward a reward (like earning game time in class)
- None

CELEBRATING SMALL MILESTONES

It is essential to recognize and celebrate the small milestones students achieve as they work toward their personalized learning goals. Acknowledging these incremental successes validates their progress and helps create and nurture a positive, supportive learning environment. Celebrating small wins also boosts students' self-esteem and motivation, reinforcing the idea that every step forward—no matter how small—is meaningful and moves them closer to their personalized learning goals.

When celebrating student progress, it is important to be mindful of the fact that students respond differently to public and private acknowledgment. Students may want to have a public celebration with their peers or might appreciate a more private celebration of their progress with a teacher or small group of friends. Charting out how students want to celebrate their incremental victories, such as in the sample chart in Figure 4.7, will help students know that the educator is truly invested in them personally.

FIGURE 4.7 • Celebrating Small Milestones Menu

INDIVIDUAL CELEBRATIONS	WHOLE-GROUP CELEBRATIONS
Personalized notes of recognition	Public acknowledgment in class
Small rewards or privileges	Showcase student work
Progress trackers	Celebration bulletin board
Phone call home with the student to share progress with their family	Group applause

STUDENT-FAMILY PARTNERSHIP REFLECTION

Fostering goal-setting habits at home involves helping children identify meaningful aspirations and breaking them down into actionable steps. For example, if a teacher observes a student struggling to stay motivated on long-term assignments, they can collaborate with the family to discuss how goal-setting is approached at home and co-develop strategies that reinforce persistence and planning. With these guiding questions, you can encourage families to reflect

(Continued)

(Continued)

on their own practices and extend a culture of purposeful growth beyond the classroom:

- What does setting a goal mean to you?
- How do we decide which goals matter most?
- What small steps help us work toward bigger dreams?
- How do we celebrate progress, even when we haven't fully reached the goal?
- How do we recover and refocus when we encounter setbacks?

As students strengthen their ability to set and pursue goals, you can gradually introduce more complex questions to deepen family conversations and build a shared language of growth and resilience.

The Big Ideas

In this chapter, we explored the significance of strategically setting, monitoring, and structuring personalized learning goals for students. The dynamic process of continually refining tasks and educational undertakings in response to each learner's advancement along their educational journey stands as a cornerstone in achieving these goals. It is imperative that these customized goals are thoughtfully aligned with the developmental stage and readiness of individual students, propelling them toward their next challenges with purpose and efficacy. Through the consistent provision of constructive feedback and proactive engagement in one-on-one goal-setting conferences, educators can ensure that these tailored objectives remain the focal point, nurturing a culture of academic excellence and progression. Moreover, the establishment of clear protocols, such as the maintenance of a designated goal-setting repository, serves to streamline this transformative process, fostering a robust framework that significantly elevates the scholarly achievements and growth of students.

Let's Reflect

Can you identify specific instances where goal-setting has positively affected students' academic performance and attainment of learning objectives?

What evidence exists to demonstrate the correlation between goal-setting and the development of students' self-efficacy and resilience in navigating academic challenges?

In what ways have the tailored goal-setting strategies contributed to students' ability to self-regulate and take ownership of their learning progression?

What's Next?

In Chapter 5, we will examine the influential practice of giving and receiving feedback. While each habit in this book has its own distinct qualities, many of them intersect and work in tandem. Chapter 5 will explicitly illustrate the integral link between goal-setting and the art of providing effective feedback. Through gaining a thorough understanding of the essential components of effective feedback, you will carefully consider the influence of "labels" on student efficacy. Negative labels have the potential to elicit defensive reactions, hindering open communication and growth. Chapter 5 also emphasizes the significance of setting up the conditions for students to receive and give peer-to-peer feedback to sustain continuous growth and achievement for all students.

CHAPTER 5

Navigate the Feedback Process

The reading class buzzed with focused energy as students revised their poetry responses, carefully considering the feedback they had received. At one table, Gabe sat motionless, his eyes fixed on the "not meeting" score at the top of his paper. The words blurred as frustration bubbled inside him. When Mrs. Evans stopped by and gently pointed out that his theme was unclear, Gabe shrugged and muttered, "I don't know how to fix it." Rather than correcting it for him, Mrs. Evans leaned in and asked a series of thoughtful, open-ended questions. Slowly, Gabe began to talk, piecing together a revised theme with her support. Encouraged but still unsure, he tried to move forward with the next part of the task—analyzing the poem's deeper meaning. Around him, classmates eagerly scribbled reflections, but Gabe hesitated, his pen hovering in midair. That familiar feeling of wanting to be rescued crept in. When Mrs. Evans circled back, she didn't offer answers. Instead, she prompted him to think aloud. "You said the rain felt like sadness and the flowers represented hope. How might those ideas work together?" With her guidance, Gabe found his voice and, for the first time, pushed through the fog of uncertainty and began to write.

WHY FEEDBACK MATTERS

It is human nature to crave feedback. Whether we are receptive to the actual feedback itself depends on various factors involved in both giving and receiving the information. The feedback process significantly impacts our efficacy and is shaped by previous experiences that affect our willingness to embrace change. We also want to know what we are doing well, particularly from those we admire. The feedback loop comes full circle as we continually move through the process, incorporating feedback that relates to previous input, building from one experience to the next.

Feedback is crucial for learning, acting as a catalyst for growth, motivation, and encouragement. One of the most influential impacts of feedback is reinforcement and cues, with an effect size of 1.01 (Hattie et al., 2024). This is because reinforcing students' efforts and providing cues to aid their next steps in learning boosts student performance. Resilient learners, therefore, proactively seek feedback, contrasting with less resilient learners, who may adopt a more passive stance. This distinction between active and passive participants underscores students' readiness to embrace the feedback process.

Feedback also relies heavily on safety and trust, which are essential to the feedback loop. Without a sense of safety, students tend to remain passive regarding feedback. As Stone and Heen (2014) link "safety" and "feedback" in their book, *Thanks for the Feedback*, they highlight that when we feel unsafe, judged, or threatened, our ability to absorb and process feedback diminishes significantly and leads to us to becoming defensive and less open to learning. In order to build the safety net of feedback, trust has to be in place. How often is academic truth conveyed when trust is absent? Human connection plays a vital role in building trust and fostering a positive feedback experience. In her book *Kids These Days*, Carrington (2019) emphasizes that all relationships ultimately hinge on connection. Building trust in the feedback process requires open communication, respect, consistency, and authenticity. Without these elements, learners will become passive participants of feedback.

Building trust among students so they can give and receive feedback is incredibly important in the classroom. Teaching them how to provide constructive feedback to one another fosters a supportive learning environment. Many share a popular quote by Zig Ziglar: "FEAR has two meanings: 'Forget Everything And Run' or 'Face Everything And Rise.' The choice is yours." This promotes the importance of students learning to navigate the feedback process so they can rise to the learning occasion (Figure 5.1).

FIGURE 5.1 ● Characteristics of Feedback

EFFECTIVE FEEDBACK IS . . .	EFFECTIVE FEEDBACK IS NOT . . .
• Being clear and specific.	• Giving vague advice or general praise (e.g., "Good job!").
• Motivating learners to improve and make changes.	• Demotivating and causing disregard to change.
• Targeting a goal or next step.	• Lacking a clear purpose.
• Building upon strengths and skills by taking an asset-based approach.	• Highlighting weaknesses or deficiencies (deficit-based).
• Using a co-constructive mindset.	• Being evaluative through judgments and measurement of results only.
• Staying rooted in a learner-empowered purpose.	• Managing a learner and their purpose.

Adapted from Prendergast and Lee (2024).

DECODING FEEDBACK TYPES

Feedback flows in all directions: from teachers to students, families to students, students to each other, and students back to teachers as well as families. Recognizing the various forms of feedback is crucial, along with understanding each type's advantages and disadvantages. A commonality across all feedback is that generic feedback falls short. Constructive feedback must be specific, clear, and, most of all, timely. Research about the immediacy of feedback (Feedback – Timing = effect size of 0.89) shows it has a limited duration and will eventually become less relevant; as students delay, the value of the feedback diminishes (Hattie et al., 2024).

When a learner proactively approaches the feedback experience with a purpose, engages intentionally with others, and applies the feedback to their work, they gain confidence in their ability to navigate each day as its own exciting learning opportunity

(Prendergast & Lee, 2024). Therefore, understanding the various categories of feedback can lead to more easily navigating the feedback process (Figure 5.2).

FIGURE 5.2 • Categories of Feedback

	CHARACTERIZED BY	PURPOSE
Promote	• Listening, questioning, paraphrasing, probing, processing, withholding judgment • Mutual brainstorming, clarifying, deciding, goal-referencing, actionable, ongoing	• Coach and collaborator • Student-centered decision-making (what students currently understand and can do) • Promoting ongoing reflection in order to expand/sharpen knowledge, skills, and capability • Generate ideas and strategies to solve instructional problems, apply and test shared ideas, and learn together • Name cognitive and metacognitive strategies
Praise	• Recognition, encouragement, gratitude, consistency, future-focused	• Increase motivation • Acknowledge results, hard work, ability, knowledge, and effort in order to motivate and thank
Persuade	• Giving advice or suggestions, directness • Modeling and demonstrating, recording tangible ideas for recipient	• Inform about details regarding tasks, procedures, content, techniques, and events
Perceive	• Observing actions • Judging • Commenting • Measuring	• Evaluate progress and results for significance • Performance based on the moment

Adapted from Brueggeman (2022).

Whether used by teachers or students, these feedback categories offer a helpful framework. The "Perceive" category involves passive behaviors such as observing, judging, commenting, and measuring. In contrast, the "Promote" category emphasizes more active engagement, including listening, asking questions, and brainstorming.

FEEDBACK TO FOSTER RESILIENT LEARNERS

Giving feedback is more than just a comment or isolated event. Before we learn how to give feedback to students or to teach them how to give it to each other, we have to instill active and supportive listening into the feedback process. Here are action steps that begin with listening:

1. Model active listening.
2. Be givers and receivers of feedback.
3. Use feedback that is strengths-based.

ACTION STEP 1: MODEL ACTIVE LISTENING

Listening plays a critical role in every part of the feedback process. It is essential not only for those receiving feedback but also for those delivering it. In conversations, it's natural to focus on what we would do, what solution to offer, or how best to respond. However, meaningful feedback begins when we listen to understand—not just to reply.

One approach to modeling active listening is to integrate a listening process into your classroom. Cornelius Minor (2019) outlines three phases of listening in his book *We Got This*, summed up by the words *hear, think,* and *ask*. The first phase is the act of listening itself—hearing. The second phase involves thinking about what we heard and striving to understand. In the third phase, we ask questions, which involves more listening. This part of the process helps anyone take the assumptions out of what a learner needs.

Ultimately, active listening is not a one-and-done step. It requires modeling repetitively and giving students multiple opportunities to practice. Consider how you model being an active listener by the evidence you collect from students about the classroom structures and routines, or in your daily behaviors. Explore opportunities with students to promote how they can be better listeners with each other. Figure 5.3 provides a list of ideas that you can use to promote active listening for all learners.

FIGURE 5.3 • Ways to Promote Active Listening

EVIDENCE TO FOSTER STUDENT INTUITION
Student survey data
Student achievement data
Student observations
Interviews or conversations (Consider even eating lunch with students on occasion!)
OPPORTUNITIES TO CULTIVATE BETTER LISTENING IN STUDENTS
Class meeting discussions
Book clubs
Group work
Partner reading
Providing examples of listening characteristics
Discuss the Constructive vs. Destructive Group Behaviors (Figure 3.2, Chapter 3)
How to be a good listener during presentations

Adapted from Brueggeman (2022).

Pause and Reflect

Think about the suggestions provided in Figure 5.3 to promote active listening as you respond to the reflection questions below.

What evidence can we use to be more intuitive with students?

____

____

____

What opportunities can we use to promote being better listeners with students?

____

____

____

ACTION STEP 2: BE GIVERS AND RECEIVERS OF FEEDBACK

It is essential to incorporate conversations about the effective characteristics of giving and receiving feedback. Consider characteristics that are outlined in Figure 5.4. While many of these traits apply to both the giver and receiver, most of the responsibility lies with the receiver. That is why it's so important to help students learn how to take in feedback. Even the most skillfully delivered feedback will have limited impact if the receiver is not prepared to absorb and act on it. Thus, teaching students how to receive feedback is the key that unlocks deeper learning. Rather than pushing feedback onto them, we must empower them to pull it in.

> Creating pull is about mastering the skills required to drive our own learning; it's about how to recognize and manage our resistance, how to engage in feedback conversations with confidence and curiosity, and even when the feedback goes wrong, how to find insight that might help us grow. It's also about how to stand up for who we are and how we see the world, and ask for what we need. (Stone & Heen, 2014, p. 6)

FIGURE 5.4 ● Characteristics of Giving and Receiving Feedback

CHARACTERISTIC	GIVER	RECEIVER
Coach	✓	
Role model	✓	
Open to ideas		✓
Choices		✓
Seeks relevance		✓
Listener	✓	✓
Reflective	✓	✓
Positive	✓	✓
Collaborator	✓	✓
Innovator	✓	✓
Seeks growth	✓	✓
Problem-solver	✓	✓

ACTION STEP 3: USE FEEDBACK THAT IS STRENGTHS-BASED

The purpose of strengths-based feedback is to build on existing positive attributes, skills, processes, and effort to encourage further growth and development. The approach falls into the "Promote" and "Praise" categories of feedback (see Figure 5.2). It is about focusing on what is working well and highlighting strengths while brainstorming the next steps. Focusing on strengths can create a more positive and less defensive environment for feedback, making the learner more receptive to improvement. There are two main processes you can use when incorporating strengths-based feedback with students.

Option 1 (Sweeney & Harris, 2017)

1. **Clarify:** Inquire with clarifying questions or statements and delve deeper to uncover additional details, successes, and challenges.
2. **Value:** Celebrate the work and highlight strengths, processes, and actions.
3. **Uncover Possibilities:** Set a goal and outline next step(s).

Option 2 (Brueggeman, 2022)

1. **Recognize:** Build on assets, skills, and processes that recognize hard work and effort.
2. **Brainstorm:** Co-construct ideas to increase knowledge, skills, and capability that promote ongoing reflection.

Both processes involve co-constructing ideas to increase knowledge, skills, and capability while encouraging ongoing reflection through choices. Some commonalities with options 1 and 2 are that they value and recognize steps use similar language, as well as they uncover possibilities and brainstorm steps. A key difference is that with option 1, clarifying questions start the process, whereas questions are embedded throughout both steps in option 2. Figure 5.5 provides language stems that will help teachers and students communicate more effectively, whether it's teachers guiding students or students supporting one another.

FIGURE 5.5 • Strength-Based Feedback Language Stems

	TEACHER	STUDENT
Clarifying at the Beginning of Option 1's Feedback Process	• Tell me more about your thinking behind (action or thinking). • Can you walk me through the process you used for . . . ? • What were your goals for . . . ? • What were some of the challenges you encountered?	• Can you explain a bit more about why you chose to . . . ? • What was your favorite part about . . . ? • What was something you found difficult?
Value or Recognize Statements	• I noticed how effectively you (positive action), which resulted in (positive outcome). • You clearly put a lot of thought into . . . • That's a great approach because . . . • You have a strong understanding of . . .	• I can see you worked hard on . . . • The way you (skill) was . . . • Good work using . . .
Uncover Possibilities or Brainstorm Statements	• Some steps you could take to further develop this could be . . . • Based on this success, you can also try . . . • The resource or support that might be helpful for you is . . .	• What's one idea you could try differently next time? • What is one thing you learned that you could use again?
Clarifying Questions at the Value or Recognize Step	• What contributed to your success? • Why did that strategy work for you? • What steps led you to . . . ?	• Why did you try that strategy? • How were you able to be successful?
Clarifying Questions at the Uncover Possibilities or Brainstorm Step	• What strategies will you use? • What resources or support would be helpful?	• How could you change . . . ? • What are other ideas you can try? • What do you expect to happen next?

Brueggeman (2022).

FEEDBACK AS A TWO-WAY STREET

Skills students need to develop the feedback process require going deeper into the art of giving and receiving feedback. This feedback can be teacher-to-student, student-to-student, or student-to-teacher. Peer feedback is a valuable method that allows students to learn from each other and expand the classroom's instructional capabilities beyond just the teacher. Furthermore, feedback provided by students to teachers is instrumental in helping educators refine instruction and better meet student needs. The effectiveness of two-way feedback is marked by mutual trust and collaboration. Building trust between students and teachers requires open communication, respect, authenticity, and consistency. When learners trust teachers and peers, they are more likely to be receptive to feedback, motivated to improve, and feel secure.

Key considerations for making feedback a two-way street include . . .

- **Timing:** It is important to deliver feedback as promptly as possible so that it is fresh in the students' minds and feels relevant to their learning.
- **Mode:** The mode of feedback delivery can pay a significant role in how students understand the information. Sometimes written feedback is better, while other times verbal feedback is necessary.
- **Consistency:** Being consistent with feedback helps create a predictable and supportive learning environment.
- **Student Agency:** Providing students with opportunities to take control over the feedback process can build independence and agency. This can involve having students reflect on their own work before receiving feedback from you or their peers. Another option is to let students choose when and how they receive feedback from others, which also provides an opportunity to practice active listening skills such as maintaining eye contact, nodding, and asking questions in an appropriate manner.

To effectively participate in this two-way street of feedback, learners need to be open to these essential pieces. Let's consider Maggie, for example, and how she yearned for feedback and discovered how she and her classmates could work together to give each other timely feedback.

FROM THE LENS OF A STUDENT

Maggie's Unexpected Wisdom From Peer Feedback

Maggie had a passion for writing and took pride in crafting every sentence with precision. That's why, when she submitted her first English assignment and received no immediate feedback, she felt a growing sense of unease. The next assignment only deepened her uncertainty—how could she improve if she didn't know whether her foundation was solid?

She wasn't alone. Her classmates felt it too. But that didn't ease Maggie's anxiety. The silence around her ungraded essay left her unsure and searching for direction. She wondered how she could move forward without knowing if her foundations were strong and secure.

Finding herself yearning for feedback in some way, she shared her next draft with classmates. Their varied perspectives—honest, diverse, and supportive—offered the clarity she needed. In working together, they discovered that peer feedback wasn't just helpful—it was essential. It became something they carried with them into future classes.

Many educators fail to give feedback in a timely manner because of the mounds of work to grade. Maggie found a solution to her need for immediate feedback in reaching out to others besides her teacher. How can we create trust for learners to give and receive feedback by teaching students how to reach out and ask for feedback from more than just their teacher? Consider working with students to be collectors of voices beyond the teacher's desk. Utilize the tools on the next page (Figures 5.6 and 5.7) to assist students in determining whom to ask for feedback and in generating effective questions when seeking feedback.

FIGURE 5.6 ● Be a Collector of Feedback—Elementary

WHOM TO ASK	OPTIONS OF AREAS OF PRACTICE FOR USEFUL FEEDBACK	AREAS OF WHAT YOU AIM TO IMPROVE	CONNECTION TO THE PROVIDER'S EXPERTISE	ADD AN OPEN-ENDED QUESTION
Teachers	Learning new skills Need to learn Goals and next steps Working with others	*I am working on writing more details in my stories so they are exciting.*	*I remember when you taught us how to add describing words to our writing, and I want to make my story as interesting as the example you showed us.*	*What do you think I did well in, and what can I work on next?*
Peers	Goals and next steps Looking at work together Using what we learned to do new tasks	*I am working on telling the steps I take when I solve a math problem.*	*I remember you were really great at telling us about your science project on plants. Can you help me?*	*How did you make it so clear for all of us to understand?*

Adapted from Prendergast and Lee (2024).

FIGURE 5.7 ● Be a Collector of Feedback—Secondary

WHOM TO ASK	OPTIONS OF AREAS OF PRACTICE FOR USEFUL FEEDBACK	AREAS OF WHAT YOU AIM TO IMPROVE	CONNECTION TO THE PROVIDER'S EXPERTISE	ADD AN OPEN-ENDED QUESTION
Teachers	Skill development Specific learning Intentions Goal-setting and next steps Collaborative group work	*I am working on improving the connection between the success criteria and the areas of improvement.*	*I remember the lesson you led us through, and I thought your examples were exactly what I hope to create for my next steps.*	*Can you tell me what strengths and growth areas you see in my work?*
Peers	Goal-setting and next steps Assistance examining work Implementation of assigned strategies and learning targets	*I am working on showing my thinking with the math word problems.*	*I remember the ratios and expressions word problems, and your example made a lot of sense to me.*	*Can you guide me in adding my explanation to this word problem about proportions?*

Adapted from Prendergast and Lee (2024).

TAMING THE TRIGGERS OF FEEDBACK

Certain factors may cause learners to ignore feedback. According to Stone and Heen (2014), there are three types of triggers: identity, truth, and relationship. Being aware of these triggers is vital, as any of them can cause students to disengage and disregard feedback. The triggers do not always relate to the person providing the feedback or the information itself. "Recognizing potential triggers and adjusting the feedback delivered can increase the potential for the feedback to be received and integrated" (Hattie et al., 2024). Let's examine what the triggers are more closely.

- **Identity Trigger:** This occurs when feedback challenges a student's sense of self, competence, or values. They might feel their intelligence or worth is being questioned.
- **Truth Trigger:** This arises when the feedback itself seems inaccurate, unfair, or irrelevant to the student. They might simply disagree with the information or process.
- **Relationship Trigger:** This is when the student feels a lack of trust, respect, or connection with the person giving the feedback. They might choose to disregard some or all of the feedback.

Based on the specific triggers that cause students to disregard feedback, there are solutions that can be supportive of students as they display certain behaviors or reactions. Figure 5.8 on the next page provides strategies to address each type of trigger, as well as supportive language and an explanation of the benefit of using each strategy. By being aware of these triggers and applying the recommended solutions, you can foster a more positive and effective feedback loop, resulting in enhanced student learning and growth.

FIGURE 5.8 • Strategies to Address Triggers

TRIGGER TYPE	LEARNER PERSPECTIVES	SOLUTIONS	LANGUAGE	BENEFITS
Identity Trigger	"I always get bad grades in math. I'm just not a math person." "This assignment shows I'm a bad writer." "The teacher thinks I'm lazy."	**Focus on effort and process:** Highlight specific strategies used and progress made. **Frame feedback as a growth opportunity:** Emphasize that feedback is meant to help them improve. **Find the appropriate setting:** Provide private feedback to avoid embarrassment.	"I noticed you took the approach . . . , and here's another option." "As writers, we are always striving to improve clarity for our readers. The introduction could benefit from a clearer thesis statement to showcase your thinking." "Tell me your plan for . . . ."	• Willingness to try again • Improved self-efficacy • Shift from fixed to growth or innovative mindset
Truth Trigger	"I spent hours on this, and you gave me a C?" "This feedback doesn't make sense. I followed the instructions." "The rubric was unclear."	**Focus on specifics and examples:** Refer to parts of student's work and share reasoning. **Ensure learners understand expectations:** Offer opportunities for clarification of rubrics/criteria. **Connect feedback to learning objectives:** Ask students to self-assess.	"The first piece of evidence supports your explanation, which supports an *almost there* on the rubric. To get a *meeting*, you need a second piece of evidence that also supports your explanation." "Explain what you think a *meeting* looks and sounds like for this success criteria."	• Greater acceptance of feedback • Improved understanding of expectations • Increased trust in the feedback process

TRIGGER TYPE	LEARNER PERSPECTIVES	SOLUTIONS	LANGUAGE	BENEFITS
Relationship **Trigger**	"The [teacher or peer] doesn't like me, so they always give me bad feedback." "They don't know what they're talking about." "They're always negative."	**Build positive relationships:** Show genuine interest in students. **Deliver feedback respectfully and empathetically:** Avoid sarcasm or harsh language. **Focus on the work:** Use strengths-based feedback.	"During our last discussion, I didn't hear from you. Is there anything I can do to make it easier for you to share your thoughts next time?" "I see that this task is challenging. What strategies have you tried so far, and how can I support you in trying a different approach?"	• Increased receptiveness to feedback • Improved relationships • Greater willingness to seek help

Pause and Reflect

Think about the triggers and correlating strategies provided in Figure 5.8. Brainstorm further ideas for feedback remediation based on current situations, past experiences, or specific students.

What is the current reality and perspectives of a student or group?	
What solutions and language will support feedback remediation?	

Labeling students also negatively impacts the feedback process, at an effect size of –0.61 according to Hattie's Visible Learning research (Hattie et al., 2024). Labeling can lead to any of the triggers, consequently leading learners to neglect feedback, which in turn disrupts the learning process. Negative labels can trigger defense behaviors, while positive labels can boost self-efficacy.

Consider shifting your view of labeling to promoting high expectations of all students and promoting students to do the same. "Students need to have higher expectations for themselves in order to be confident and open to learning" (Brueggeman 2022, p. 114). Student estimations of their learning are usually not far off from reality. Interestingly, Hattie's research on the MetaX website shares that the strategy "Self-Reported Grades" has a 0.96 effect size (Hattie, n.d.b). If students understand what is expected and receive effective feedback, they know if they are going to be successful when performing. This aligns with their mindset of growth and learning. "Receiving feedback, when rooted and framed in a learner-empowered mindset, is not only highly impactful but is also entirely within your realm of control as to how, when, and why to receive that feedback" (Prendergast & Lee, 2024, p. 106).

The evaluations we make regarding students establish our expectations and the way we give feedback, consequently determining the conditions for their success or failure. These assessments represent a teacher's appraisal of a student's academic achievement. On Hattie's list of effect sizes, teacher estimates of achievement is at a 1.29 effect size. It is defined as follows:

> **Teacher Estimates of Achievement:** The estimates of student achievement made by teachers. These teacher judgments can help set expectations, be used to benchmark past understanding, are involved in setting the next challenges, help identify those who may have early signs of difficulties, inform placement and intervention choices, and influence instructional choices. These judgments can come from questioning, observing, written work, presentations, how the student reacts to increased challenge, and assignments and tests. (Hattie, n.d.d)

It is mind-blowing to realize that our estimates shape our expectations of students and can significantly impact their achievement! This means we need to adjust our expectations for all students. We have to put aside our biases and expect that all students can learn and meet expectations through the feedback process. We also need to understand that the heavy lifting is on learners as well. So that means we have some work to do to guide our students to maintain appropriately high expectations for each other. Ellen, currently an assistant principal, recounts how she used several methods to create a safe and structured environment when she was a fifth-grade teacher, to ensure that every learner engaged in the feedback process. Discover how she integrated strategies and routines from the beginning of the school year, resulting in a class full of advocates.

FROM THE LENS OF A TEACHER

How Ellen Helped All Students Find Their Voice Through Feedback

The hum of a new school year always carried a familiar hope: that every student would feel seen and heard. Feedback was a cornerstone of learning in every subject and moment in Ellen's classroom each year. Ellen's goal was to encourage participation from more than just the same five students, ensuring that all voices contributed and felt valued. They started with class meetings focused on the basics of giving and receiving feedback, modeling how to offer simple noticings—"I noticed you held the door open for our class as we came back in from recess"—to demonstrate that feedback was more than just "You're nice." Ellen also incorporated a compliment sticks routine. Students wrote compliments on index cards to each other and collected them on key rings. As the school year went on, they progressed to giving compliments about effort in math or insightful reflections in science, and so on. Students always had criteria to guide their feedback, both for peers and for their own reflection. They also learned hand signals for agreement and disagreement and practiced carrier phrases, like "Can you explain?" or "An option is . . . ." This supported effective dialogue whenever students engaged in the feedback process. The key was active engagement from everyone; it was an expectation from the start. In the end, all students were equipped with a life skill.

Modeling the use of giving and receiving feedback is another important step Ellen took regularly. Like Ellen, keep in mind how to use language in your conversations with your scholars that will push students further to believe in themselves and increase their efficacy along the way. Encourage your colleagues to do the same. For example, ask yourself and colleagues, "How can we build positive relationships with students who struggle with feedback triggers?" Also, try promoting student-facing questions, such as "How can we build positive relationships with peers who struggle with feedback triggers?" Using specific behavior-focused language, avoiding labels, encouraging reflection, and providing support, teachers can create a trusting and less triggering environment for students, essential for daily feedback navigation.

CONNECTION

Refer to Chapter 6 for more about questioning and Chapter 7, as it connects expectations to a learner's mindset.

STUDENT-FAMILY PARTNERSHIP REFLECTION

To encourage students to seek feedback from family members, emphasize the unique perspectives their loved ones can offer by having students and families discuss the topic of feedback. Class meetings are an opportunity to highlight that family members can support them in learning new strategies, reviewing their learning, and even helping them understand the teacher's expectations. Share the following Student-Family Partnership Reflection questions with students and their families to help guide them in having feedback conversations.

- What kind of support from our family would help you collect more information or try out new skills or strategies at home?
- How can we reinforce learning or better understand feedback, and what kind of encouragement or discussion would be most helpful?
- How do you figure out what teachers expect from you in your schoolwork and your learning behaviors?

As you considered these questions in earlier chapters, think about asking students and families to share their reflection conversations during the annual parent-teacher conference or school event.

The Big Ideas

This chapter highlights how to actively engage students in the feedback process, rather than act as passive recipients. Feedback is a powerful learning tool that requires students to be resilient and seek it out. We examined various feedback forms, including teacher-to-student, student-to-student, and student-to-teacher feedback. A key aspect discussed was teaching essential skills for giving and receiving feedback, such as active listening, empathy, constructive criticism, open-mindedness, and co-creation of ideas. Trust is also vital for effective feedback and can be fostered in a positive, supportive classroom. We also addressed the impact of labels in feedback, emphasizing the need to avoid them and focus on specific behaviors to reduce defensiveness. Ultimately, cultivating a feedback-valuing culture empowers students in their learning journey.

Let's Reflect

How are you fostering trust within your learning environment to ensure students feel safe and respected enough to both give and receive feedback openly?

What criteria are you using to select the type and language of feedback to prevent triggering behaviors or causing negative effects from labels?

What are some ways you might integrate strengths-based approaches into your practice?

What's Next?

Chapter 6 leads us through the process of helping resilient learners uncover their capacity to endure challenges. We will examine barriers and student indicators to support students using an asset-based approach to dispel deficit thinking. You will see how to create a classroom where perseverance becomes a cultivated skill by strategically scaffolding and encouraging students to develop their own supports. This approach helps students gain confidence in facing challenges, equipping them with the tools and self-awareness needed to navigate complexities and achieve their goals.

CHAPTER 6

Persevere Through Obstacles

Keegan and his classmates looked forward to story time each day, eagerly gathering on the carpet after lunch. With wide eyes and active imaginations, they listened as Mr. Stuever brought characters to life with every turn of the page. They laughed, asked questions, and even acted out scenes, treating the stories like old friends. But everything changed when Mr. Stuever shifted from reading aloud to teaching reading skills. The joy Keegan felt began to fade. Letters seemed to swim on the page, turning words into confusing puzzles. He hesitated, stumbled, and grew quiet. Even though he knew some friends were also finding it tough, Keegan couldn't stop the voice in his head whispering, "This is too hard. I'll never read." His confidence cracked each time he misread a word or forgot a sound. Watching another student effortlessly read through a whole book made his heart sink. "That kid's just smarter than me," he thought. "Better at everything." It wasn't just about reading anymore—it felt like a reflection of his worth. Still, he kept showing up, clutching his book tightly, hoping that one day the jumble of letters might finally begin to make sense.

WHY PERSISTENCE MATTERS

In today's intricate educational landscape, the ability to persevere through obstacles stands as a cornerstone of student success. Experiencing challenges is a part of life. In a world full of complexities, students who can keep their motivation high and stay focused, even when facing setbacks, are truly better prepared to tackle challenges and reach their goals. This capacity to push through difficulties is not merely a desirable trait but a critical skill that empowers learners to thrive. Learners who view challenges as opportunities for growth and learning, rather than insurmountable roadblocks, are more likely to achieve success.

Closely related to perseverance is the concept of grit, which encompasses not just the ability to persist through challenges but also a sustained passion and commitment to working toward long-term goals. Author and researcher Andrea Duckworth (2016) shares, "To be gritty is to keep putting one foot in front of the other. To be gritty is to hold fast to an interesting and purposeful goal. To be gritty is to invest, day after week after year, in challenging practice. To be gritty is to fall down seven times and rise eight" (p. 5). Just as grit involves sticking with things over the long haul, perseverance enables students to work through immediate obstacles as well as over time in pursuit of their learning objectives. Furthermore, cultivating a learning mindset that embraces difficulties as part of the learning process directly supports the development of perseverance. As Carol Dweck (2016) says, "The passion for stretching yourself and sticking to it, even (or especially) when it's not going well, is the hallmark of the growth mindset" (p. 7).

However, children are often surrounded by messages and experiences that link mistakes to failure, inadequacy, or negative outcomes. This can cause them to view mistakes negatively rather than as opportunities for learning. Research indicates that many children develop a significant fear of failure, which can stem from various sources, like setting unrealistically high standards or societal pressure to succeed. A recent study indicated that children showed an increased fear of making mistakes when their emotions were not acknowledged and discussions about setbacks were absent (Peterson et al., 2024). By analyzing their mistakes and developing strategies to avoid similar errors, resilient students cultivate the persistence needed to overcome hurdles.

Additionally, the stigma associated with failure in many cultures can make children feel ashamed and reluctant to acknowledge their errors (González Jurado-Gutiérrez, 2024). Research by Brené Brown and others highlights the damaging effects of shame on learning and development. As Brown (2021) shares, "shame is the intensely painful feeling or experience of believing that we are flawed and therefore unworthy of acceptance and belonging" (p. 143).

When children experience shame regarding their mistakes, they tend to internalize the error as a judgment of their self-worth, interpreting it as "I am bad," instead of recognizing it as a specific action, "I have made a mistake." By viewing mistakes as stepping stones to embrace opportunities for growth and innovation, students develop resilience and are empowered to persevere through complex tasks, ultimately fostering independence and self-awareness in their learning journey (Figure 6.1).

FIGURE 6.1 • Characteristics of Perseverance

PERSEVERANCE IS . . .	PERSEVERANCE IS NOT . . .
• Maintaining effort and focus despite encountering setbacks.	• Avoiding challenges and searching for the easy way.
• Pushing through difficulties.	• Giving up easily when faced with difficulties.
• Analyzing mistakes to identify areas for improvement.	• Accepting the current level of skills and knowledge.
• Developing strategies to avoid the same struggles.	• Repeating actions without reflecting on obstacles.
• Embracing challenges as opportunities for growth and learning.	• Being hindered by a fear of failure.
• Forming an integral part of a learning mindset.	• Lacking the ability to analyze our learning mindset.

UNDERSTANDING BARRIERS AND EMBRACING THE ASCENT

Achievement rarely follows a smooth path. It is often filled with obstacles that test even the most dedicated individuals. Understanding the barriers that hinder students from embracing these challenges and maintaining persistence is crucial to fostering a generation equipped to navigate complexity and achieve their full potential. Figure 6.2 outlines barriers affecting students' perseverance and provides indicators for students to identify when these barriers impact them. The aim is to equip students with self-awareness.

FIGURE 6.2 • Barriers to Perseverance and Corresponding Student Indicators

BARRIER TO PERSEVERANCE	STUDENT INDICATORS
Fear of Failure	• Avoiding challenging tasks or situations where you might not succeed immediately • Feeling anxious or worried about making mistakes • Giving up easily when something becomes difficult • Procrastinating on tasks you're unsure about • Focusing more on the outcome (getting it right) than the learning process • Being overly self-critical when you do make a mistake

(Continued)

(Continued)

BARRIER TO PERSEVERANCE	STUDENT INDICATORS
Fixed Mindset	• Believing your abilities are set and can't change much • Thinking "I'm just not good at this" when faced with difficulty • Avoiding challenges because you don't want to look "dumb" • Feeling threatened by the success of others • Giving up quickly when you encounter setbacks • Being less receptive to feedback or criticism
Unknown Expectations	• Feeling confused or unsure about what you're supposed to do • Feeling overwhelmed by the task without clear direction • Hesitating to start a task because you're not sure where to begin • Feeling frustrated because you're putting in effort but not seeing results • Avoiding asking for help for fear of looking uninformed • Feeling a lack of control over your progress
Lack of Motivation/ Interest	• Feeling bored or uninterested in the task • Struggling to find the energy or drive to work on it • Prioritizing other activities over the challenging task • Questioning the relevance or purpose of the task • Feeling a lack of personal connection to the goal • Experiencing difficulty focusing or staying engaged
Overwhelm/ Burnout	• Feeling stressed, tired, or emotionally drained • Having difficulty concentrating or focusing • Feeling like you have too much to do and not enough time • Losing interest in things you usually enjoy • Experiencing physical symptoms like headaches or fatigue • Feeling a sense of hopelessness or cynicism about the task
Lack of Effective Strategies	• Trying the same approach repeatedly, even when it's not working • Feeling stuck and unsure how to move forward • Not knowing where to find resources or support • Feeling like you're working hard but not seeing progress • Giving up because you don't know how to tackle the problem • Not breaking down large tasks into smaller, manageable steps
Negative Self-Talk	• Having critical or discouraging thoughts about yourself and your abilities • Telling yourself you can't do it or that it's too hard • Focusing on past failures or negative experiences • Doubting your capacity to succeed • Comparing yourself negatively to others • Feeling like you're not smart enough or capable enough

Start the journey of this habit by creating opportunities for students to increase their awareness of the internal and external factors that hinder their perseverance. By understanding these barriers, students can begin to shift their perspectives and develop the resilience needed to embrace challenges and persist through obstacles. Consider the list as options to support learners, and as the chapter progresses, we will explore strategies to help learners address these challenges.

- **Self-Reflection:** Encourage students to regularly reflect on their thoughts, feelings, and behaviors when faced with challenges.
- **Identify Potential Barriers:** Use the "Student Indicators" column in Figure 6.2 to help students identify which barriers might be at play.
- **Seek Support:** Encourage students to discuss these indicators with teachers, counselors, or trusted adults.
- **Strategize:** Once a barrier is identified, students can brainstorm ways to overcome the barrier.

FROM THE LENS OF A STUDENT

Cecelia's Approach to Turning Challenges Into Opportunities for Growth

Cecelia felt aimless in high school as she and her middle school friends drifted apart. Yearning for connection, Cecelia nervously joined the cross-country team despite having no running experience. Before her first race, she was filled with nerves. "What if I don't do well? What if I can't keep up? What if I'm not good enough?" That first race was humbling. Cecelia finished near the back, feeling sore and discouraged. Unlike the successes in other areas she had enjoyed before, this activity was definitely a struggle. Though doubt tried to creep in, her dad's encouraging words and the support from her friendly team kept her spirits up and pushed her forward. Cecelia committed to learning, analyzed her stride, and attended every practice. Slowly, improvements came. Her times dropped, and her racing became more assertive. While not the fastest, Cecelia was beating her own records, a deeply satisfying achievement. Cross-country unexpectedly gifted her perseverance in other areas of her life. Her violin practice became consistent, and her academic work improved. She embraced the fears as learning opportunities. Before running, Cecelia hadn't grasped the meaning of perseverance. Now, it shapes her approach to challenges, making her more diligent and thoughtful.

CONNECTION

In Chapter 7, you will dive deeper into vulnerability and explore how to create a culture of questioning that also supports perseverance.

Cecelia truly learned a valuable lesson about perseverance! Instead of focusing on deficits and shortcomings exposed by challenges, encourage learners to identify and leverage their existing strengths, resources, and prior experiences to navigate difficulties. Taking an asset-based approach offers a powerful counter-narrative to these barriers. Drawing on the work of psychologist Saleebey (2013), a strengths perspective emphasizes the inherent capacity within individuals and communities. Rather than viewing mistakes as failures that expose limitations, this approach recognizes them as valuable data points that can be leveraged for future growth and success. In essence, overcoming the shame associated with mistakes is a critical step in adopting an asset-based perspective (Brown, 2012). When we are less afraid of judgment and more willing to be vulnerable about our errors, we can more effectively analyze them for their learning potential and build the perseverance needed to try again.

Take the time to encourage students to recognize their existing capacity for perseverance. By doing so, this fosters a sense of agency and empowers them to approach future challenges with a more positive and resourceful mindset. Use the following perseverance reflection activity, Identifying and Activating Assets, to help students embrace an asset-based approach to persevering through obstacles.

IDENTIFYING AND ACTIVATING ASSETS

1. **Identify Past Challenges:** What is a significant challenge you successfully overcame in the past (academic, personal, or extracurricular)?
2. **Recognize Strengths and Resources:** What specific strengths, skills, and resources helped you navigate that challenge? (e.g., determination, problem-solving skills, support from friends or family, specific knowledge, or past experiences)
3. **Acknowledge Learning:** Identify what was learned from that experience, both about the challenge itself and one's capabilities.
4. **Connect to Current Obstacles:** How can the strengths, resources, and lessons learned from past success be applied to a current obstacle?
5. **Develop an Action Plan:** Create an action plan that outlines some specific steps to tackle the current obstacle, using the positive aspects identified as the foundation.

Embracing the ascent, though demanding, is where true learning and development occur. It is in navigating the complexities and pushing through discomfort that students discover their own capabilities and develop the grit necessary for long-term success.

Pause and Reflect

Go through the steps of identifying and activating assets yourself. How did personally engaging with this process deepen your understanding, and what can you share from your own journey as an example for your students?	
What specific details or adjustments do you need to make to inform how you introduce or facilitate the activity with your students?	
How can this activity be leveraged to help students better understand barriers to perseverance and embrace the ascent?	

CULTIVATE AN INNOVATIVE LEARNING MINDSET

Cultivating an innovative learning mindset is a crucial step in empowering students to become not just learners but also proactive problem-solvers and creators in an ever-evolving world. Building upon the foundations of perseverance and an asset-based perspective, an innovative mindset encourages students to move beyond simply acquiring knowledge to actively seeking new solutions and approaches. Building off of the work of Carol Dweck and George Couros, this involves students increasingly taking ownership of their learning journey and taking essential steps toward growth and innovation. Carol Dweck's (2014) growth mindset approach suggests that abilities, intelligence, and talents can be developed, leading to new ideas:

> Mindset change is not about picking up a few pointers here and there. It's about seeing things in a new way. When people change to a growth mindset, they change from a judge-and-be-judged framework to a learn-and-help learn framework. Their commitment is to growth, and growth takes plenty of time, effort, and mutual support. (p. 244)

The three components of growth—time, effort, and support—encourage genuine learning. To add to that, George Couros's (2015) characteristics of an innovator's mindset—empathetic, problem finders, risk-takers, networked, observant, creators, resilient, and reflective—are essential for creating meaningful learning experiences for everyone. A logical progression to get to the highest levels of learning mindset can be seen in this way: fixed, emerging, growth, and innovator. Utilizing the combined thinking of Couros and Dweck, Figure 6.3 shares definitions and characteristics of each learning mindset component as well as outcomes that a learner may showcase as a part of each mindset.

Learners will likely have different mindsets based on various experiences and factors, such as reading compared to math. Transitioning from a fixed mindset to one of growth and innovation focuses more on the journey than constantly being an innovator. More so than anything, it is about encouraging learners to step outside of their comfort zone—be comfortable with being uncomfortable in their learning (Brueggeman, 2022). Among other benefits, Nowik (2025) shares that as learners grow, they will have a desire to challenge themselves more, and their self-confidence will increase when they take steps outside of their comfort zone.

Adding to the goal-setting work of Chapter 4, we can also have students set goals for their learning mindset. Embracing a growth and innovative learning mindset signifies a progression toward greater independence and a proactive engagement with the complexities of learning. A tool to help students is the Learning Mindset Progression and Success Criteria shown in Figure 6.4. Begin by having students reflect on the category

FIGURE 6.3 • Learning Mindset Definition and Characteristics

	DEFINITION	CHARACTERISTICS	LEARNER OUTCOMES
Fixed Mindset	Abilities, intelligence, and talent are constant.	• Avoids challenges • Gives up easily • Effortless • Ignores feedback • Feels threatened by others' success • Seeks completion	A learner will maintain their mindset, which will be lower than their full potential.
Emerging Mindset	Abilities, intelligence, and talent are unbalanced.	• Uncertain about risks • Anxious • Inconsistent effort • Varies with feedback • Follower • Seeks acceptance	A learner may make slight increases in the attainment of knowledge or skill.
Growth Mindset	Abilities, intelligence, and talent can be developed.	• Embraces challenge • Persistent • Effort equals mastery • Learns from feedback • Inspired by others' success • Seeks perfection	A learner will gain knowledge and skills and/or reach high levels of achievement.
Innovator's Mindset	Abilities, intelligence, and talents can be developed, leading to the creation of new and better ideas.	• Empathetic • Problem-solution finders • Risk-takers • Reflective collaborators • Flexible experimentation • Passionate • Seeks improvement	A learner will be empowered to seek creativity and be a critical thinker.

Adapted from Brueggeman (2022), Couros (2015), and Dweck (2016).

they mostly fall into, and then have them select one or two of the criteria to help them move into the next category closer to growth and innovator.

FIGURE 6.4 ● Learning Mindset Progression

FIXED	EMERGING	GROWTH	INNOVATOR
The learner is accepting of the current mindset and will maintain skills and knowledge without questions or risk-taking.	The learner is uncertain about attempting new skills and may work little by little to make small improvements.	The learner is inspired to increase achievement and is persistent in mastering new skills.	The learner is empowered to attempt to solve new problems and is passionate about improving critical thinking skills while being flexible with next steps.

Success Criteria:

- I can set a focused goal and revise when needed.
- I can listen to feedback and take action in attainable steps.
- I can try out something new in manageable chunks.
- I can make time to ask questions and be creative.
- I can celebrate the easy and difficult steps in my practices.

Brueggeman (2022).

THE INFLUENCE OF EXPECTATIONS ON A LEARNER'S WILLINGNESS

Similarly to Chapter 5, where we discussed the importance of expectations in relation to feedback, expectations significantly influence students' perseverance. Our beliefs regarding the learning process intrinsically shape these expectations, which often stem from our own past performances and tend to be very subjective. For example, a teacher may have the perspective that their students will all magically learn and understand a skill the first time they teach a concept, based on their ability to teach a lesson or past lesson results. Our unclear communication of expectations can further contribute to students' difficulties in embracing challenges and maintaining persistence. Ultimately, teacher expectations greatly impact student achievement, with an effect size of 0.58 (Hattie, n.d.e).

A teacher can also inadvertently let biases affect their expectations for students. High expectations stem from the belief that not holding all students to high standards denies them quality education, as student achievement correlates directly with expectations (Samuels, 2020). Our judgments of students' readiness and/or abilities ultimately set learners up for success or failure. Furthermore, many educators struggle to communicate expectations effectively while also providing adequate support for students tackling complex tasks independently. This implies that if expectations are not communicated clearly or if the support provided does not align with those expectations, students may find it more challenging to persevere.

How can we shift our expectations from subjective judgments to informative judgments? Let's take Joe, a STEM teacher in Pennsylvania, for example. He acknowledges that learning is not always easy for his students and that embracing the struggle is a part of the process, setting the precedent that he expects students to productively struggle. Setting high expectations encourages students to develop grit and the understanding that learning often involves overcoming obstacles. He learned that his high expectations of struggle were not always clear to the students, and it took time and patience with some learners to progress in their ability to work through challenges. Read how his true empowerment lies in helping students become independent learners, not in handing over the answers.

FROM THE LENS OF A TEACHER

How Joe Witnessed Student Struggle

The lively STEM lab revealed a stark contrast to the general classroom, highlighting the value of struggle. Joe observed two student responses to challenges. Some would immediately declare defeat, echoing the pleas for answers he had witnessed before in reading and math: "I don't understand!" or "This is just too hard!" His response shifted to prompting reflection: "What have you tried?" and "Show me your work." These simple prompts often acted like a key, transforming the struggle into a starting point for learning.

The second type of learners were students who persevered on their own, teaching Joe a new approach to problem-solving along the way. He recalled when they were building structures to test engineering design principles, one student ingeniously used testing stick material flexibility for structural support against wind in an unconventional way that surprised him. It wasn't in the resources, and it wasn't what he had demonstrated, but it worked! These moments underscored the importance of celebrating those alternative solutions and making the process visible to the entire class.

Joe was, in essence, building self-regulated learners who take ownership of their learning. Scholars should maintain high expectations for themselves, but they must regularly reassess their goals and plans with support if needed. There is a direct correlation between the importance of having higher expectations and growing our mindset about learning. To visualize that correlation, let's revisit the balance between a fixed and an innovator's mindset as it relates to "expectations" using the diagram shown in Figure 6.5. If learners expect more of themselves, are forward-thinking, and are willing to take the time to learn, then they are more apt to be innovative and successful. With higher expectations come more fruitful results.

FIGURE 6.5 ● Learning Mindset and Expectation Tug-of-War

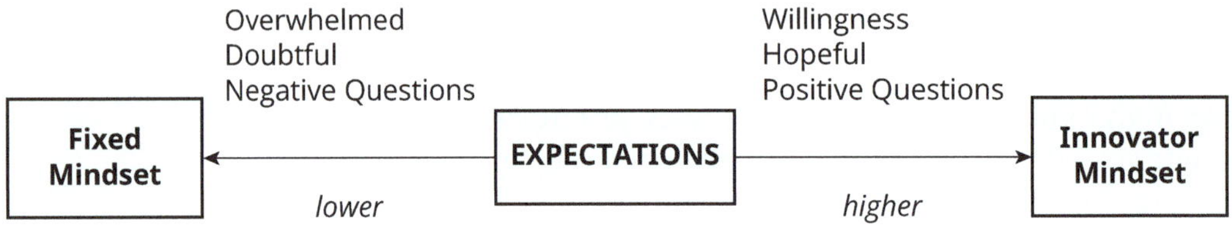

Brueggeman (2022).

Family expectations can also influence a learner's willingness to engage with challenges. At a 0.49 effect size, parental expectations refer to the perceived level of aspirations that parents have for the academic success of their students (Hattie, n.d.a). As educators, we can assist families and students by proposing home-use strategies that highlight persistence. These include emphasizing the problem-solving process instead of merely seeking the correct answer, celebrating efforts (regardless of correctness), and viewing mistakes as opportunities for learning. Refer to the Student-Family Partnership Reflection at the end of the chapter for questions to also support conversations outside of school.

STRATEGIC SCAFFOLDING TO SUPPORT PERSEVERANCE

As adults, we naturally grasp how some items or processes are needed in navigating our daily lives. We set reminders for appointments, utilize timers and to-do lists, and break down large projects into smaller, more manageable steps. How many of us have thought that those are scaffolds that help us stay organized and focused, and ultimately, help us persevere through our responsibilities? Actually, those are resources because they are long-term tools we naturally go to in order to stay on top of it all.

What is the difference between a resource and a scaffold? In the educational context, scaffolding refers to the temporary supports that educators provide to students to bridge the gap between their current abilities and the desired learning outcomes (Bruner, 1978). Scaffolds, or supports, are gradually removed as students gain independence and mastery. Resources are broader, used long term, and used repeatedly to support a variety of learning tasks.

Unfortunately, teachers often either under-scaffold or over-scaffold, struggling to find the right balance for their students. Under-scaffolding causes students to blame themselves for failures instead of recognizing the lack of support (Smith et al., 2024). When teachers over-scaffold, students do not experience productive struggle; instead, they encounter over-helping, which can lead to dependence on the teacher, a reduced rigor in lessons, and a belief among students that their teacher has limited faith in their capabilities (Smith et al., 2024). In order to start the process of implementing strategic scaffolding, it takes understanding three key characteristics (Finley, 2025):

- Contingency
- Fading
- Transfer of responsibility

Figure 6.6 provides scaffolding strategies based on the different categories and fosters effective support from the teacher side and increased ownership from the student perspective.

Examples of scaffolds that transcend all categories could include checklists, graphic organizers, visual aids, sentence stems, and modeling. Here are some tips to remember when using scaffolds:

- Offer a range of scaffolding options.
- Teach students how to use scaffolds.
- Encourage students to support each other.
- Gradually release responsibility.
- Encourage self-reflection.

FIGURE 6.6 • Scaffolding Strategies for Teachers and Students

CATEGORY	TEACHER ACTIONS	STUDENT ACTIONS
Cognitive: Supporting learners in gaining new skills or understand concepts	• Share ideas by thinking aloud during problem-solving. • Chunk information into smaller, more digestible parts. • Ask targeted, guided questions to prompt deeper thinking.	• Find ways to structure thinking and understanding. • Ask clarifying questions when unsure about concepts. • Explain concepts to others to grow and solidify understanding. • Chunk information into smaller parts.
Metacognitive: Supporting learners in planning, monitoring, evaluating their own learning	• Facilitate discussion about effective learning strategies. • Guide students in goal-setting and time management. • Provide opportunities for students to self-assess.	• Set learning goals and monitor progress. • Make plans in how to approach tasks before starting. • Reflect on the learning process and experiment to find effective strategies. • Identify areas of strengths and possible next steps.
Procedural: Supporting learners in using the steps required to complete tasks	• Break down complex tasks into sequential and manageable steps. • Establish clear routines and procedures for classroom activities. • Teach students how to use available resources.	• Follow step-by-step instructions carefully. • Identify and access necessary resources and tools. • Learn and follow classroom routines. • Seek clarification when needed. • Organize materials and workspaces effectively.

As students gain a better understanding of their learning needs, motivate them to formulate their own support strategies. This may include crafting personalized checklists, designing their own graphic organizers, or pinpointing useful online resources.

HARNESSING THE POWER OF COLLABORATIVE INQUIRY

When you think of collaborative inquiry cycles from the teacher's perspective, it involves analyzing student data of any kind and guiding subsequent steps. There are several types of

FIGURE 6.7 ● Levels of Student Involvement in Collaborative Inquiry

Collaborative Inquiry Process (Option 1) 1. Powerful predictions 2. Purposeful observations and exploration 3. Thoughtful explanations 4. Measured action Prendergast and Lee (2024)		
STUDENTS AS PASSIVE PARTICIPANTS	**STUDENTS AS CO-PARTICIPANTS**	**STUDENTS AS FACILITATORS**
1. I wonder if students are . . . 2. I see that students are . . . 3. What does past history say about . . . ? 4. Set a goal and an action plan.	1. We wonder if . . . 2. We are surprised that . . . 3. What do we know about previous attempts to . . . ? 4. Co-create the plan: What will we do and by when?	1. We predict . . . 2. Some patterns/trends are . . . 3. We need to collect additional information on . . . 4. Co-create the plan: How can we make our goal measurable so that we can achieve it?
Collaborative Inquiry Process (Option 2) 1. Identify a student learning need. 2. Develop a focused goal. 3. Complete a short inquiry. 4. Decide one to three action steps. 5. Review end results and celebrate. Brueggeman (2022)		
STUDENTS AS PASSIVE PARTICIPANTS	**STUDENTS AS CO-PARTICIPANTS**	**STUDENTS AS FACILITATORS**
1. Students are . . . 2. Students will . . . 3. Review 4. Give students "look-fors" when . . . Help students make a plan for . . . 5. Students are . . . Students love . . .	1. Brainstorm with students about a current class need. 2. Co-create a goal. 3. Guide students on who, what, and where to research. 4. Co-create the action plan. 5. Students reflect and share the end results.	1. Have a system for students to bring up learning needs. 2. Co-create a goal. 3. Students complete open-ended research for action steps. 4. Co-create the action plan. 5. Students reflect and share the end results.

collaborative inquiry processes, but we include two options that are student-centered and are a problem-solution based approach. Option 1 is a four-step process to approach conversations using predictions and data observations. The second option includes five steps where setting a goal based on student learning needs is the driver for the inquiry. As you explore the two processes shown in Figure 6.7, reflect on the roles students play in a teacher's collaborative inquiry cycle. One approach is that students are passive participants. Another idea is to consider students' increased involvement in the process at varying levels. Both options and progression of student involvement support scholars in persevering through learning challenges.

STUDENT-FAMILY PARTNERSHIP REFLECTION

Emphasizing the problem-solving process and viewing mistakes as opportunities is a mindset shift for families as well as students. By acknowledging the high expectations we set for learners as a systematic process that involves persistence, we can model for families the value of the learning mindset. Consider the options provided in the previous chapters, or explore alternative methods to engage students and families through these reflective questions.

- How do we respond when something is hard or we make a mistake?
- What hopes and dreams do we have for the learning journey?
- How can we create a supportive environment that encourages effort and resilience?
- What helps us keep trying even when things are tough?
- How do we communicate expectations?

Recognizing perseverance and progress in overcoming barriers can be challenging for learners. Think about ways to encourage students and families to celebrate those moments. It can make everyone feel appreciated and motivated to keep creating wonderful learning memories together that lead to a deeper level of student motivation in the classroom environment.

The Big Ideas

In this chapter, you have discovered that the ability to persist amid difficulties distinguishes resilient learners. You examined barriers and student indicators to support students using an asset-based approach to dispel deficit thinking. Scholars recognize that obstacles can become stepping stones for personal and academic growth. By strategically scaffolding and encouraging students to develop their own supports, educators foster a classroom where perseverance transforms into a cultivated skill. This helps students gain confidence in facing challenges, equipped with tools and self-awareness to navigate complexities and reach their goals.

Let's Reflect

What are some ways you can help students overcome barriers to perseverance?

____

____

____

How can you encourage a growth and innovative learning mindset with students?

____

____

____

What evidence do you currently use to identify moments when students are demonstrating resilience or struggling to persevere, both as a class and as individuals?

____

____

____

In what ways can you rethink scaffolding to help students build the confidence, strategies, and mindset needed to navigate challenges independently over time?

____

____

____

What's Next?

In Chapter 7, we will discuss vulnerability and how to encourage students to express their thoughts, question assumptions, and build on one another's ideas. This habit will dive deeper into ways to foster this active engagement by cultivating a culture of questioning. Navigating productive struggle with directional supports will also be introduced as a reinforcement of the notion that vulnerability is not a weakness but a strength in the learning process.

?
X + Y = ?

CHAPTER 7

Embrace Vulnerability

In a kindergarten classroom, during a discussion about the life cycle of a butterfly, Jack raises his hand, his brow furrowed in thought. With a slight hesitation, he asks, "But . . . but how does the caterpillar know to go into the sleepy shell?" This simple query opens the door for the teacher to explain the chrysalis and encourages other young learners to voice their own uncertainties without fear of judgment.

Across the district, in a high school business class engaged in a discussion about market research, Allie tentatively raises her hand. The class has been exploring different methods of gathering consumer data. Allie, after listening to a classmate confidently explain the benefits of online surveys, asks, "While online surveys seem efficient for reaching a large audience, could relying heavily on them create a bias in our data? Are we missing the perspectives of demographics who may not have consistent internet access or who are less likely to respond to online questionnaires?" Allie's question delves into the potential limitations and ethical considerations of a seemingly straightforward business practice, revealing a willingness to question the presented information and acknowledge a gap in her understanding of potential biases.

In both classrooms these moments of questioning highlight the power of vulnerability in learning. Jack's query and Allie's interrogation represent students taking risks to show vulnerability, a fundamental aspect of becoming resilient, lifelong learners.

THE IMPORTANCE OF VULNERABILITY IN LEARNING

Vulnerability plays a crucial role in fostering effective learning environments by encouraging students to actively engage with the information and take intellectual risks. Resilient learners are characterized by their willingness to be vulnerable, moving beyond being passive recipients of information to become active participants in their own learning journeys. A key element of this active participation is the willingness to ask questions. Questions are one of the most powerful ways students express their thinking, enhance problem-solving, monitor understanding, and improve as active and autonomous learners (Lara-Alecio et al., 2012). By creating opportunities for students to articulate their thoughts and challenge assumptions, educators are promoting inherently vulnerable acts that lead to deeper understanding and the development of critical thinking skills.

Embracing vulnerability in learning is directly linked to creating a culture of questioning within the classroom. As Ron Ritchhart (2023) shares, fostering student curiosity and questioning involves creating opportunities for authentic problem-solving and robust inquiry. Unfortunately, many of these conditions are all too rare in schools today, according to Ritchhart. It's quite unfortunate that we frequently notice a gap in the productive struggle and a lack of rich learning environments. Ritchhart goes on to share that many teachers tend to value answers at the expense of encouraging students to ask good questions. Students who actively formulate their own questions about a lesson subsequently outperform those who merely restudy the material by 33 percent, according to a study comparing the effects of generating questions (Ebersbach et al., 2020).

Research also emphasizes that when students are free from worries about being judged or humiliated, they are more likely to engage with the material and participate actively in discussions, ultimately fostering deeper learning. As Danielson et al. (2024) note, "When a strong culture for learning and a respectful, safe environment are present, classroom discussions engage all students in important issues, provide opportunities for critical thinking, deepen and extend understanding, and promote the use of precise language" (p. 77). Therefore, cultivating an environment where vulnerability through questioning and open dialogue is valued and encouraged is fundamental to creating resilient, lifelong learners (Figure 7.1).

FIGURE 7.1 • Characteristics of Vulnerability

VULNERABILITY IS . . .	VULNERABILITY IS NOT . . .
• Taking risks in order to learn.	• Being a passive recipient of information.
• Willingness to ask meaningful questions.	• Resembling monologue more than dialogue.
• Embracing a factor that can enhance engagement.	• Being done only by the teacher or adult.
• Being an active participant in the learning journey.	• Prioritizing answers over encouraging questioning.
• Articulating thoughts and being open to hearing other voices in discussions.	• Being present in classroom discussions where not all students are engaged.

LEVERAGING DIRECTIONAL SUPPORTS FOR PRODUCTIVE STRUGGLE AND QUESTIONING

Imagine your students as learners navigating their own educational journey. Just like Dorothy needed support in *The Wizard of Oz*, learners benefit from different kinds of support to feel confident and successful in their learning environment. Think of these support options as helping scholars find the right path in their learning "forest" (Figure 7.2). It's important to recognize that this journey will inevitably involve challenges where students encounter productive struggle. This suggests that learning is most effective when it is challenging but not too difficult, pushing learners to the edge of their capabilities to foster cognitive growth (Hammond, 2024b).

By understanding these different areas of support and assisting students to analyze them, it is easier to identify needs leading to success in the learning journey. It is important to note that needing support in more than one area at a time is common. As we uncovered barriers to perseverance in Chapter 6, it is essential to reiterate that students may struggle due to frustration or feelings of being overwhelmed by vulnerability as well. Providing emotional support involves teaching them the importance of embracing vulnerability in learning and that struggle is a regular and valuable part of the

FIGURE 7.2 ● Directional Supports

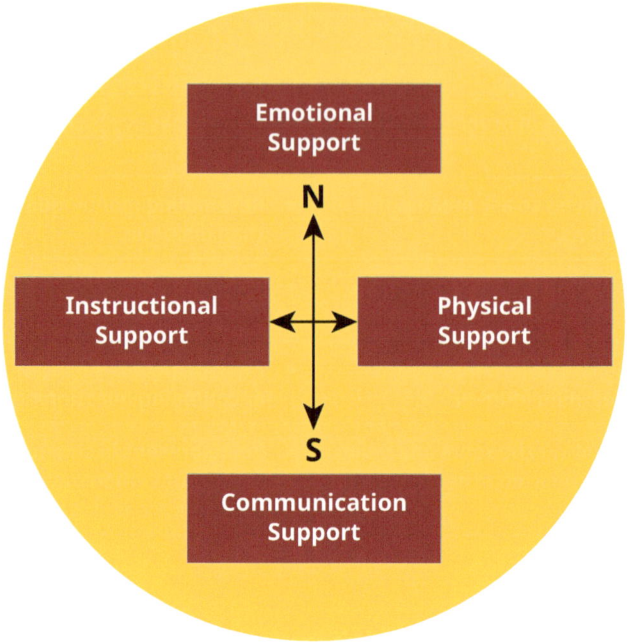

Brueggeman (2022).

process. This includes understanding that the brain thrives on challenge and learns from mistakes (Hammond, 2024b). By understanding that it's OK to not know immediately, guided by their North, students might be more willing to engage in productive struggle. "We have to help students find the joy in deliberate practice and productive struggle," (Hammond 2024b, p. 49).

Using Figure 7.3, let's take a closer look at the four areas of directional support—emotional, communication, physical, and instructional—to be able to provide guidance that helps learners navigate the challenges of productive struggle more effectively. The chart can be introduced to students as it is and adapted over time. As we continue through the chapter, you will collect ways to encourage students to ask clarifying questions within these support structures as a powerful tool for resilience.

FIGURE 7.3 • Summary of Directional Supports

EMOTIONAL	COMMUNICATION	PHYSICAL	INSTRUCTIONAL
North Star! Emotional support encompasses health and overall well-being as a learner. It includes • Paying attention to your social-emotional needs, • knowing and understanding your trauma, • feeling emotionally safe and supported in a classroom, and • allowing productive struggle not to get the best of you.	*South!* Communication support is about connections and communication in the school environment. It includes • interactions with other students, • ways you communicate with teachers, • understanding expectations, both from teachers and family, • navigating team collaboration, and • asking and answering questions	*East!* Physical support involves materials and procedural parts of the student environment. It includes • knowing where resources are located in the school and classroom, • understanding routines and schedules, and • how the classroom is set up.	*West!* Instructional support entails how we are taught and how we learn best. It includes • choosing appropriate methods and instructional strategies to meet your needs, • observing how other students learn, • discussing your learning and progress, and • taking ownership of your learning and developing your critical thinking skills.

Adapted from Brueggeman (2022).

FOSTERING PSYCHOLOGICAL SAFETY THROUGH COMMUNICATION

A significant interconnectedness exists among communication, emotional support, and the establishment of a learning environment wherein students are afforded the security necessary to pose questions and embrace intellectual risks, ultimately cultivating trust and psychological well-being. For any human, the words we choose to use and listen to have the incredible ability to lift us up or hold us back from achieving our true potential and growing in amazing ways. Think back to giving and receiving feedback in Chapter 5. The words used have either been helpful to students in their learning journey, or at other times the messages have deeply wounded them and possibly prevented growth (Prendergast & Lee, 2024).

The same can be said for unspoken language, if not to an even greater extent. Nonverbal communication has the power to foster or hinder a safe space for learners and also relates back to expectations from Chapter 6. In high-expectation classrooms, the emotional climate is caring and nonthreatening (Rubie-Davies, 2014). Facial expressions, posture, gestures, breathing, eye contact, and tone all play an important role in how students feel and engage in the learning environment.

Modeling appropriate vulnerable behaviors, both verbal and nonverbal, is crucial for building trust and making students feel safe. Consider, for example, how we think out loud or show forgiveness. "Being vulnerable with kids and sharing when you might need to restate something or apologize for how you said something shows students you are a reflective and empathetic teacher" (Prendergast & Lee, 2024, p. 45). Use the Directional Supports chart (Figure 7.2) to describe a learner's perspective, specifically narrowing in on the Emotional Support category. Another modeling option is to refer back to the academic identity work (Chapter 1) or Be a Collector of Feedback (Chapter 5). Have students revisit the impact of different influencers in relation to the directional supports, specifically communication. Encourage students to think about how the words of others have positively or negatively impacted their academic identities. For an additional approach, read Summer's reflection on her experiences with her history class of high school juniors, which shows how students taking the risk to show vulnerability can lead to greater clarity.

FROM THE LENS OF A TEACHER

Summer's Approach to Fostering Psychological Safety

Recently, Summer's class was learning about government assistance, and a student, hesitantly, asked, "Don't most Black families get welfare?" It was a moment of vulnerability for the student who spoke up, but many students leaned forward, interested in hearing more. Instead of just giving an answer, they used a graph that broke down the data by age and gender as well as ethnic groups. They even compared it to government involvement in other countries, like Russia, as they looked at some images. That "small" question, seemingly born from a misconception based on their community make-up, moved learning forward in major ways. It highlighted the power in questioning, not just by Summer, but also by students. It reminded Summer that her role is to foster an environment where students feel safe to ask questions and discuss hard topics, and that it is expected and valued. As Summer thinks back to how she set the stage for moments like this, she knew it was because she always aims to build relationships. Monday meetings were one way for her to get to know students and set the stage for sharing on a personal level. The environment in which students feel free to have conversations matters, so they don't think twice about opening up when it comes time to learn more deeply.

Pause and Reflect

How can you intentionally use both your verbal and nonverbal communication to create a classroom environment where students feel safe to ask difficult questions and engage in vulnerable discussions?

____

____

____

What routines or practices might you implement to strengthen relationships with students and signal that their voices and experiences are valued in our shared learning journey?

____

____

____

BELONGING AS THE BRIDGE BETWEEN COMMUNICATION AND PSYCHOLOGICAL SAFETY

Psychological safety in the classroom does not happen by accident. Rather, it is cultivated through deliberate actions that signal to students that their voices, identities, and experiences are not only accepted but valued. At the heart of this safety is a sense of *belonging*, the belief students hold that they are seen, heard, and respected as integral members of the learning community. When students feel they belong, they are far more likely to participate, take academic risks, and persevere through challenges—all hallmarks of a resilient learner. This is why fostering belonging must be a central priority for teachers committed to building psychologically safe environments.

The way teachers communicate with students plays a critical role in shaping that sense of belonging. Warm, affirming language, active listening, and intentional modeling of vulnerability all help students feel emotionally supported and cognitively engaged. Even simple phrases like "I'm glad you're here today," or "That's a great question! I hadn't thought of it that way," can signal to students that their presence and contributions matter. Conversely, when students perceive communication as dismissive, critical without support, or inconsistent, it erodes trust and heightens anxiety, reducing the likelihood that they will engage fully.

Creating a culture of belonging is not the same as creating a space where students are always comfortable. It's about creating a space where they feel safe enough to be *authentic*, even when learning is hard. It's about knowing they can ask questions, make mistakes, and try again without fear of judgment or ridicule. As described in *Student-Centered Mentoring* (Brueggeman, 2022), a strong mentor mindset prioritizes relational trust and models how to navigate setbacks with empathy and perspective. Teachers who embody this mindset position themselves as allies in the learning journey rather than as critics of performance. This encourages students to speak up, reach out, and stay engaged.

It's also important to remember that the culture of a classroom is defined not by rules posted on a wall but rather by how students feel within it. When teachers prioritize communication that fosters trust and build routines that affirm students' identities, they create classrooms where resilience can take root. Students who feel they belong are more likely to embrace intellectual risk, reflect on feedback constructively, and persist through challenges—not because they are told to, but because they know they are supported in doing so. Belonging, then, is not a soft goal—it is the foundation on which both psychological safety and deep learning are built.

Whether we are building relationships as a community by getting to know each other better as a class, or starting conversations about what is happening in the community, we, as teachers, must model vulnerable thinking first. Here is a list of concepts that can be used with learners at any age to model and engage in discussions about vulnerability:

- Model how to restate something out loud.
- Apologize for how you said something.
- Describe an experience related to the Directional Supports topics (Figure 7.2).
- Revisit the Sample Academic Identity Impact Chart (Figure 1.3).
- Review the Be a Collector of Feedback charts (Figures 5.6 and 5.7).
- Display movie clips for students to analyze verbal and nonverbal communication cues.
- Discuss presentation techniques and audience behavior.

In order to set the stage for questioning with any discussion, activity, or protocol, setting questioning norms and expectations will be key for the safety of all students. For elementary school students, questioning norms should emphasize nurturing curiosity and building a foundational understanding that it is acceptable to seek clarification. In secondary schools, norms shift in focus toward critical thinking, respectful debate, and prioritizing evidence-based reasoning. Figure 7.4 outlines the focus, provides examples, and gives the underlying goal of supporting psychologically safe communication for students.

FIGURE 7.4 ● Questioning Norms and Expectations Features

	PRIMARY	SECONDARY
Focus	• Curiosity • Basic understanding • Normalizing lack of knowledge	• Critical thinking • Respectful disagreement • Evidence-based reasoning
Examples	• It's OK to say "I don't know" and ask for better understanding. • Respectful listening • "Are you sure?" can be asked to help us think more	• Focus on ideas, not people in disagreements • Challenge assumptions respectfully • Allow think time • Build on each other's ideas
Underlying Goal	• Build confidence in asking basic questions and participating	• Develop skills in analysis, evaluation, and constructive dialogue

CULTIVATING A CULTURE OF QUESTIONING

Creating a classroom where questioning is expected, valued, and rewarded is essential for a thriving learning culture. When teachers consistently ask thoughtful questions, they demonstrate the importance of inquiry and provide a framework for students to follow. Whether the questions are surface-level or delve into the depths of learning transfer, content-based questions, as well as skill and strategy-based questions, are all valuable. It is also crucial to focus on encouraging student-initiated questions. Further, "New demands in the workplace strengthen the imperative that all students leave the school with the ability to ask questions, collaborate on teams to solve problems, and develop respectful relationships with those who think differently or look different" (Walsh & Sattes, 2017, p. 3). Let's take Destiny, a student from Miss Turner's eleventh-grade U.S. Government course, as an example of how students can learn to consistently ask meaningful questions, leading them to be comfortable taking risks and engaging in deeper learning.

FROM THE LENS OF A STUDENT

Destiny's Comfort with Questions

Stepping into Miss Turner's class has never made Destiny nervous. Learning about Lincoln and the Jim Crow laws felt huge, but she was never worried about getting things wrong or forgetting. Miss Turner has a way of making it OK to not know everything. When Destiny asked a question about segregation and shared her thinking, it probably wasn't right. But Miss Turner didn't just say, "You are wrong." Instead, she said, "You might be right, but let's think more about that."

"It's like she knows we're taking a risk just by speaking up. It's not always about right or wrong with her. Miss Turner doesn't just stand at the front; she walks around, helping everyone, whether we are the 'honors' students or not," Destiny said. Destiny found herself asking, "What does this mean?" a lot, or "How does this help me learn better?" and even, "What can I do to improve?" Asking those questions actually makes things clearer. It's like Miss Turner is helping them see that being vulnerable enough to ask questions is how they actually learn and understand things better. Teachers like Miss Turner make a difference to Destiny.

As we prepare scholars like Destiny, consider the range of questions we can incorporate into our language on a daily basis. Keep in mind how to use questioning in your conversations with your colleagues that will push students further to believe in themselves and increase their efficacy along the way. Then, support students in incorporating the language that will push them to using questions more frequently. Figure 7.5 provides sample questions that teachers can ask each other and students can use to support a culture of questioning in the classroom.

FIGURE 7.5 ● Questions That Support Both Teachers and Students

QUESTIONS FOR TEACHERS TO ASK EACH OTHER	QUESTIONS FOR STUDENTS
• What do we envision our low and high expectations of learning should be? • How can we push learners to go higher than their own expectation? • Are we equitable when it comes to our expectations of students? • What do we expect the student outcomes to be? • How do we think all students will perform? • How can we build a classroom culture where mistakes are seen as learning opportunities? • How can we build positive relationships with students who struggle with triggers? • How can we make rubrics and learning objectives more student-friendly?	• How do we self-assess ourselves using rubrics, learning objectives, etc.? • How can we build positive relationships with peers who struggle with feedback triggers? • What strategies can we use to better understand expectations and learning objectives? • How do we learn to feel safe to take risks, identify our strengths, and learn from mistakes? • What strategies can we use to demonstrate respect and empathy of our peers?

Adapted from Brueggeman (2022).

To further cultivate a culture of questioning, educators can implement structured discussions that encourage students to articulate their thoughts and challenge assumptions. Student-led discussions, as research suggests, can lead to overall increased student participation in classroom conversations and exercises, as well as higher satisfaction and emotional investment in learning (Kurczek & Johnson, 2014). According to Hattie et al. (2024), the influence of classroom discussion and formal discussion are both at a 0.82 effect size, which shows that either inviting students to interact with peers informally or formally greatly influences their learning as well. Figure 7.6 provides some examples to consider embedding into the classroom on a regular basis.

FIGURE 7.6 • Student-Led Discussion Options

INFORMAL DISCUSSIONS	
DISCUSSION ACTIVITY AND PROTOCOL	**HOW CAN THE DISCUSSION PROCESS BE MORE STUDENT-LED?**
Small Group Buzz Session 1. Divide students into small groups. 2. Generate a focused question or topic. 3. Have each group engage in an informal discussion.	Instead of the teacher generating a focused question or topic, try having students brainstorm and submit questions or topics prior to the activity.
Pop-Up Debate 1. Present a statement or issue with two clear sides to students. 2. Have students quickly choose a side. 3. Instruct students to circulate around the room and pair up with someone who chose the opposite side. Then have students present their arguments.	Instead of the teacher creating a statement or issue, try having the class compose a list of issues and sides related to the topic at the beginning of a unit and occasionally bring one of the ideas up as a pop-up debate.
FORMAL DISCUSSIONS	
Socratic Seminar 1. Before • Choose a text. • Prepare open-ended questions. • Annotate text. • Set up the room and the activity expectations (e.g., form inner and outer circles). 2. During • Facilitate the discussion. • Extend and challenge ideas. 3. After • Reflect on the learning. • Debrief about the process.	Instead of the teacher extending and challenging ideas, try having the class make notes as they annotate to be prepared to extend and challenge during the seminar.

Now that you have examined the opportunities described in Figure 7.6, use the Pause and Reflect box to brainstorm other ideas for how to increase the level of student-led discussions in both informal and formal discussions.

Pause and Reflect

What is the activity that you are thinking of outlining?

___

___

___

How can the discussion process within that activity be more student-led?

___

___

___

How might you embed more questions that support a culture of questioning with your students?

___

___

___

ENHANCING ENGAGEMENT THROUGH VULNERABILITY

Connecting vulnerability to active participation in learning is crucial to foster resilient learners. This willingness to be vulnerable is a cornerstone of active engagement, as it pushes students beyond passive reception of information toward actively seeking understanding, which you will explore even further in Chapter 10. According to Zaretta Hammond (2024b), fostering internalization of information requires engaging students in "productive

CONNECTION

Refer back to Chapter 3 for ideas on how to prevent common problems when implementing student-led discussions, and brainstorm ways to implement solutions as challenges come up.

struggle" with challenges, even with little to no support, to spark cognitive growth. This process inherently involves vulnerability, as she goes on to share that students confront the limits of their current knowledge and understanding—their zone of proximal development—through desirable difficulties.

The act of questioning reflects a willingness to be vulnerable about what they don't understand, which, in turn, drives learners to engage more deeply with the material to find answers and clarify their understanding. It is also through successful discussions that all students are engaged, seeking the perspectives of everyone and ensuring all voices are heard, which deepens and extends understanding. As you will explore more deeply in Chapter 10, this aligns with Amy Berry's (2022) engagement continuum where students disengage when they are disrupting, avoiding, and withdrawing, and engage when they are participating, investing, and driving. Students who are "investing" or "driving" their learning are actively asking questions about what they are learning and seeking feedback, demonstrating a level of intellectual vulnerability that fuels their engagement. Have students use this reflection tool, Figure 7.7, to reflect on a challenge and their own productive struggle in relation to engagement and vulnerability.

STUDENT-FAMILY PARTNERSHIP REFLECTION

Educators can also further support modeling how to be vulnerable when having conversations with families. The questioning norms and expectations from this chapter can be communicated in various ways to students and families, such as during a curriculum night. Additionally, share and encourage the reflection questions to help students and families consider both verbal and nonverbal noticings.

- Recall a moment when you received verbal communication that either encouraged or interrupted your vulnerability.
- Describe a time when you received nonverbal communication that either motivated or hindered your desire to learn.
- How did those nonverbal and verbal examples make you feel?
- What areas of verbal and nonverbal communication would better support you as a learner?

Building a partnership between the school and families where questioning is encouraged and valued is crucial for a thriving learning culture. Consider a system or process that helps students and families feel safe asking questions, which encourages everyone to take risks and engage in deeper learning.

FIGURE 7.7 ● Student Reflection Template

REFLECTION OF MY PRODUCTIVE STRUGGLE IN LEARNING YOUR CHALLENGE	
Describe a learning task or problem that you found challenging. What made it difficult for you?	
Do you think this challenge fell into that "just right" zone for you, or was it overwhelming? Why?	
How much support did you have during this challenge? How did that impact your learning?	
YOUR ENGAGEMENT	
Where do you think you were on the engagement continuum during this challenging task?	Disrupting > Avoiding > Withdrawing > Participating > Investing > Driving
Were you actively participating in trying to solve the problem, or were you more passive?	
Did you see the purpose of working through this challenging task?	
YOUR VULNERABILITY	
At any point during this challenge, did you feel like you didn't know what to do? If yes, what was your reaction?	
Were you willing to take risks and try different approaches? Did you form your own questions about the challenge?	
Did you feel safe enough to admit if you were confused or needed help? Did you ask others questions during this process?	

The Big Ideas

This chapter emphasizes that embracing vulnerability, particularly through questioning, is essential for fostering resilient learners who actively participate in their learning. Starting with the idea of providing directional supports, educators empower students to take ownership of their learning needs. Fostering curiosity and questioning involves creating opportunities for authentic problem-solving and establishing a classroom culture where vulnerability and questioning are valued. When students consistently ask meaningful questions, they become comfortable taking risks that not only lead to learning but also develop critical skills to articulate thoughts, challenge assumptions, and build on each other's ideas. By cultivating a classroom culture where questioning is expected, valued, and rewarded, educators empower students to embrace their uncertainties, actively seek understanding, and ultimately achieve higher learning outcomes.

Let's Reflect

What are some ways you can effectively support the directional needs of students and foster psychological safety, ensuring they feel secure enough to be vulnerable in their learning?

____

____

____

How are you cultivating a classroom culture where questioning is valued and expected, allowing students to take risks and show vulnerability in their learning by asking questions, articulating their thoughts, and challenging assumptions?

____

____

____

How are you incorporating "desirable difficulties" and promoting productive struggle in lessons, helping students understand that mistakes are part of growth and encouraging them to embrace vulnerability when facing challenging material?

____

____

____

What's Next?

Looking ahead to Chapter 8 on cultivating tech-savvy scholars, we will explore both the empowering benefits of technology, such as personalized learning through AI and expanded access to educational resources, alongside critical considerations. We will also address the potential pitfalls of an overreliance on technology, including its effects on critical thinking, as well as the crucial ethical and privacy implications that must be carefully navigated to ensure responsible integration of technology.

CHAPTER 8

Develop Tech-Savvy Scholars

Emily, a middle school student, wielded technology as her trusty companion but struggled to use it for her academics. Despite having a world of knowledge at her fingertips, Emily struggled to use her device effectively. Distracted by non-educational content, she found it challenging to focus on her studies, leading to a noticeable decline in her academic performance. Worse still, her excessive screen time began to encroach upon her well-being, impeding her social interactions and overall development.

Recognizing the impact of technology on Emily's learning journey, her teacher stepped in, to help transform Emily's technology habits and help her utilize technology tools more effectively. Through structured technology breaks, the teacher encouraged moments of respite from screens, unlocking opportunities for offline activities and fostering meaningful face-to-face connections among students. With clear guidelines for technology use and a strategic integration of digital tools for targeted learning activities, the teacher artfully guided Emily and her peers to use technology more effectively and efficiently. By prioritizing their holistic development, the teacher championed a balanced approach to screen time, ensuring that the students' educational journey was enriched with both digital proficiency and social-emotional growth. The teacher's wisdom and guidance became Emily's guiding North Star, illuminating a path for her to thrive in the digital age while nurturing Emily's overall well-being.

WHY DIGITAL ACUMEN AND INTEGRATION OF TECHNOLOGY WITH STUDENTS MATTERS

In nurturing the growth of tech-savvy scholars, educators and families stand as crucial influencers in preparing students with essential digital competencies for success in today's high-tech society. By implementing comprehensive digital literacy initiatives that exceed fundamental computer proficiencies, encompassing disciplines such as coding, data analysis, artificial intelligence (AI), and digital ethics, students are empowered to adeptly leverage technology for effective navigation and utilization. Such initiatives not only build students' technical skills but also cultivate resilience in the face of the myriad challenges posed by technology, ensuring their preparedness for the complexities of the digital age they are forced to navigate.

Furthermore, integrating tools such as learning management systems and artificial intelligence allows for real-time data analysis, enabling educators to identify struggling students early on and provide targeted interventions to support their academic growth. Technology not only individualizes the learning process but also empowers learners to develop essential skills such as self-regulation, perseverance, and problem-solving, ultimately equipping them with the resilience needed to thrive in an ever-evolving digital world.

Therefore, the integration of advanced technologies like artificial intelligence into learning environments presents a transformative opportunity to meet the diverse needs of students. By integrating AI-powered tools alongside learning management systems, educators gain a powerful ally in identifying struggling learners early on and providing them with tailored support to enhance academic growth. Simultaneously, AI algorithms can be leveraged to challenge and stretch high-achieving students, ensuring that every learner receives personalized attention and experiences intellectual growth with their abilities. This blend of technology not only individualizes the learning journey but also cultivates crucial skills like self-regulation, confidence, and adaptability (Figure 8.1).

FIGURE 8.1 ● Characteristics of Tech-Savvy Scholars

TECH-SAVVY SCHOLARS ARE . . .	TECH-SAVVY SCHOLARS ARE NOT . . .
• Utilizing digital tools to enhance learning outcomes.	• Passively consuming technology without engagement in learning activities.
• Applying critical thinking skills to evaluate online information.	• Blindly accepting information without verifying its credibility.
• Collaborating with peers using online platforms for group projects.	• Using technology as a means for isolation instead of social interaction.
• Safeguarding personal data and practicing online safety measures.	• Disregarding privacy concerns and sharing sensitive information online.

STRATEGIES TO SUPPORT STUDENT TECHNOLOGY INTEGRATION

Figure 8.2 offers practical strategies to facilitate the seamless integration of technology into students' learning experiences. Educators can utilize these strategies to foster digital literacy, critical thinking, and collaboration skills, positioning students for success. After reading each strategy in the chart, reflect on opportunities where you might try each strategy, now or in the future!

FIGURE 8.2 ● Technology Integration Strategies

STRATEGIES FOR STUDENT TECHNOLOGY INTEGRATION	DESCRIPTION	AN OPPORTUNITY WHERE I MIGHT TRY THIS STRATEGY IS . . .
Digital Skills "Ed Camp"	Conduct Ed Camps (mini workshops) to enhance students' digital literacy, covering topics like online research, cyber safety, and effective use of educational apps.	
Teacher-to-Student Tech Support	Offer personalized support and troubleshooting to students navigating technological hurdles within their learning journey, ensuring tailored assistance to address their specific challenges effectively.	
Collaborative Tech Projects	Encourage students to work on collaborative tech projects that promote teamwork, problem-solving, and creativity while leveraging digital tools.	
Continuous Feedback Loop	Create mechanisms for students to provide feedback on tech tools and platforms used in the classroom, ensuring their voices shape future technology integration efforts.	
Personalized Path Tech Mentors Program	Create a mentorship initiative in which technologically adept students assist their peers in effectively navigating and utilizing educational technology tools and resources.	

FROM THE LENS OF A STUDENT

Tai Puts Artificial Intelligence to Work for His Benefit

As a student who had long struggled with reading and writing, Tai never imagined that something like artificial intelligence (AI) could transform his learning experience. At first, he was skeptical about how it might help, but using AI in the classroom changed the way he saw himself as a learner. Instead of constantly feeling behind, Tai began to feel understood.

The AI tools adapted to his unique learning needs—identifying when he needed more time, what types of explanations resonated with him, and which topics required extra support. It no longer felt like guesswork. Lessons became more personalized, allowing Tai to work at his own pace without the fear of embarrassment or being left out.

What surprised him most was how the experience sparked a sense of ownership over his learning. He stopped waiting for direction and began setting goals for himself. Over time, Tai realized he wasn't just keeping up—he was growing and improving. AI didn't simply support his schoolwork; it helped him believe in his ability to succeed.

ARTIFICIAL INTELLIGENCE: PEAKS AND PITFALLS

Integrating AI and technology into education presents myriad benefits and challenges for student learning. On the positive side, AI tools offer personalized learning experiences that cater to individual student needs and learning styles. In *Artificial Intelligence Playbook*, Meghan Hargrave and colleagues (2025) highlight the transformative power of artificial intelligence in education, emphasizing its potential to revolutionize student learning experiences. Hargrave et al. eloquently articulate, "AI has the capacity to personalize learning like never before, catering to individual student needs and enhancing educational outcomes" (p. 137). These authors' innovation and observation underscore the profound impact AI can have on education by tailoring instruction to meet the diverse learning styles and preferences of students, ultimately fostering a more engaging and effective learning environment. By analyzing vast amounts of data, AI can provide insights into student progress, enabling educators to tailor instruction effectively. Technology also enhances accessibility, breaking down geographical barriers and providing opportunities for remote learning and collaboration. Furthermore, interactive resources and simulation tools powered by AI can make abstract concepts more tangible and engaging, fostering deeper understanding and knowledge retention among students.

However, while there are a plethora of positive benefits of integrating technology, specifically AI, into teaching and learning, it is wise to be mindful of how and when we use any and all technology. Leaders, teachers, students, families, and communities must come together and rumble with how to navigate the potential challenges that may arise alongside AI and the benefits of using technology in the science of learning. Here are just a few of the potential concerns:

- **Increased screen time and digital overload:** This can contribute to attention issues and reduced face-to-face interactions among students.
- **Digital divide:** It is crucial to ensure equal access to technology for all students, regardless of their socioeconomic backgrounds.
- **Preservation of privacy and data security:** This presents significant challenges, as safeguarding student information against breaches and misuse becomes increasingly vital in the digital educational landscape.

Navigating the integration of AI and technology in education demands that educational leaders, teachers, students, and families strike a delicate balance between leveraging the advantages of technology while mitigating its associated challenges. Teaching kids how to use AI resources for their own personalized learning paths is great, but not teaching them how to be a responsible digital consumer is reckless and leaves our students extremely vulnerable. Students have access to lots of writing and mathematical AI technology. When used to help a student become more resilient in their writing, critical thinking, or problem-solving, AI is an innovative resource. However, it is paramount that we also teach students that using AI to do their writing, critical thinking, and problem-solving for them without giving credit to the AI resources can become plagiarism and is extremely problematic. Specifically, with students in middle and high schools, the integration of AI presents a double-edged sword, bringing both opportunities and challenges. While AI holds the potential to streamline academic processes and enhance learning experiences, its utilization also introduces the peril of plagiarism. With advanced AI tools capable of generating sophisticated content, there arises a heightened risk of students succumbing to the temptation of academic dishonesty. Moreover, the challenge intensifies in the case of high-stakes assessments, where the elusive nature of AI-generated content poses a significant threat to the integrity of academic evaluation. As educators, parents, and community members, it is paramount to address this challenge through a combination of comprehensive education on ethical conduct, vigilant monitoring of student work, and the implementation of sophisticated anti-plagiarism tools to uphold academic integrity in the digital age.

By integrating ethical considerations into the learning and fostering discussions on the implications of AI technology, students are equipped to make informed choices as digital consumers. Emphasizing critical thinking and digital literacy skills, educators empower students to discern credible information from potentially biased or manipulated sources. Through real-world examples and scenarios, students not only grasp the ethical dilemmas posed by AI but also develop a strong foundation for ethical decision-making in the digital realm. Ultimately, by nurturing a culture of ethical awareness and moral reasoning, educators mold students into conscientious AI digital consumers who approach technology with discernment and integrity.

Amid the transformative impact of AI on education, it has the profound potential to empower students on their personalized learning journeys, fostering resilience and adaptability. By tailoring learning experiences to individual strengths, challenges, and preferences, AI equips students with the tools to navigate obstacles with confidence and perseverance. Through personalized feedback, adaptive resources, and real-time interventions, AI enables students to actively engage in their learning process, building essential skills such as problem-solving and self-regulation. This personalized approach not only enhances academic performance but also cultivates resilience by instilling a growth mindset and a sense of agency in students, preparing them to thrive in an ever-evolving educational landscape.

By encouraging students to reflect on their experiences with AI, educators can guide them toward responsible and ethical use of technology while nurturing essential skills for a digitally driven world. Figure 8.3 shares three scenarios and reflective questions for teachers to work through with their students.

FIGURE 8.3 ● Student AI Experiences: Reflection Prompts

SCENARIO	REFLECTIVE QUESTIONS
Scenario 1: Responsible Use of AI A student, Sarah, utilizes an AI-powered study tool to enhance her understanding of complex concepts. She diligently tracks her progress and engages with the feedback provided by the AI system. However, she inadvertently becomes overly reliant on the tool, neglecting to develop critical thinking skills independently.	**Scenario 1:** Responsible Use of AI • How do you balance the benefits of AI assistance with developing your own problem-solving skills? • In what ways can you ensure that AI remains a supportive tool rather than a replacement for independent learning?
Scenario 2: Ethical Considerations Mark, a student, uses an AI chatbot to access academic assistance outside of school hours. While the chatbot offers valuable support, Mark discovers that his conversations are being stored and analyzed for research purposes without his consent.	**Scenario 2:** Ethical Considerations • How can you advocate for transparency and ethical use of AI tools in your learning experiences? • What steps can you take to protect your privacy and data when interacting with AI technologies?
Scenario 3: Digital Well-Being Jenny relies on an AI-driven time management app to schedule her study sessions efficiently. However, she notices an increase in her screen time and a decrease in face-to-face interactions with peers, leading to feelings of isolation and dependence on technology.	**Scenario 3:** Digital Well-Being • How do you maintain a healthy balance between using AI tools and fostering meaningful offline connections? • What strategies can you implement to promote digital well-being and mindfulness while engaging with AI technologies in your learning journey? • Ultimately who is hurt by overuse or misuse of technology?

FROM THE LENS OF A TEACHER

Ms. Sundaram Grapples With the Right Blend of Tech

Ms. Sundaram, a seasoned teacher, constantly struggled with the nuanced task of integrating technology into her classroom while preserving the essence of traditional teaching methods. Balancing the diverse learning needs of her students, the demands of a rigorous curriculum, and the

(Continued)

(Continued)

rapidly evolving world of educational technology, she faced the formidable task of discerning the optimal mix of tech tools to enhance learning experiences without sacrificing vital human connections and time-tested teaching practices.

Amid these formidable hurdles, Ms. Sundaram navigated the complexities with unwavering resolve and strategic acumen. One of the primary challenges she encountered was the initial resistance from some students to embrace technology in the classroom, stemming from varying levels of digital literacy and comfort with tech tools. To address this, she implemented targeted training sessions and personalized support, ensuring that all students felt empowered to engage with technology confidently.

Another significant challenge arose in managing the vast array of digital resources available, leading to potential overwhelm and inefficiency. In response, Ms. Sundaram, with the support of her peers, curriculum coach, and administration, meticulously curated a selection of high-quality tech tools that offered embedded AI supports and that aligned seamlessly with her lesson objectives. This streamlined the integration process and maximized instructional impact. Finally, Ms. Sundaram recognized the impact of screen fatigue and was very mindful in making sure students were spending the time necessary with technology while balancing it with interactive and interpersonal learning opportunities.

FROM METACOGNITION TO META-STRATEGIC THINKING

Metacognition—"thinking about one's thinking"—is a foundational skill in resilient learning. It enables students to reflect on what they know and don't know, monitor their progress, and evaluate outcomes (Flavell, 1979). However, metacognition alone does not equip students to respond strategically. As Zohar and Barzilai (2013) explain, *meta-strategic thinking* extends beyond awareness. It involves a deeper level of regulation in which learners understand what strategies they have available, how those strategies function, and when to apply or adapt them to a given learning task.

In an era of rapid change, information overload, and ubiquitous technology, students who develop both *metacognitive* and *meta-strategic* thinking become empowered learners capable not just of reflection but of making intentional, strategic decisions about their learning processes. In K–12 classrooms, this means fostering habits that help students both navigate challenges and use technology as a purposeful tool to enhance, not distract from, their learning.

For example, a student using metacognition might recognize, "I'm struggling with this math problem." A meta-strategic thinker, however, goes further: "I've used the distributive property before in similar problems—let me try that and see if it works here." This kind of decision-making reflects not only resilience but mastery of one's learning tools. It requires a learning environment where students are encouraged to think flexibly, try multiple approaches, and reflect on the effectiveness of different strategies.

THE ROLE OF TECHNOLOGY IN STRATEGIC LEARNING

Technology offers unprecedented opportunities for personalized, creative, and collaborative learning. But without guidance, students may engage with technology passively or even counterproductively—clicking through tasks, multitasking ineffectively, or relying on AI tools without understanding the learning behind them. To be resilient and strategic users of technology, students must be taught to think about how they're using tech tools and why they're using them in specific ways.

Teachers can begin by modeling their own decision-making when using technology. For instance, a teacher might say, "I'm choosing to use this graphic organizer app because it helps me organize my ideas visually before I write," or "Let's use this search engine filter to narrow down our research to credible sources." This kind of modeling highlights both learning moves and strategic tool use, which are key aspects of meta-strategic thinking (Zohar & Barzilai, 2013).

Students can also be taught to assess the affordances of different tools. When introducing a new digital resource, teachers can prompt students to reflect:

- What is this tool helping you do?
- When might it be most useful?
- Are there times when a different method might be better?

By encouraging students to think about their choices, teachers help them shift from consumers of technology to intentional users who can evaluate, manipulate, and optimize their digital learning experiences.

CLASSROOM PRACTICES THAT BUILD BOTH RESILIENCE AND STRATEGIC USE OF TECHNOLOGY

The following text outlines effective classroom practices aimed at fostering resilience and promoting strategic use of technology among students. These strategies emphasize explicit instruction, goal-setting, problem-solving, productive struggle, and collaborative projects, all integrated with digital tools to enhance student learning experiences. Notice how each strategy specifically supports student development of other habits within the book, too! By incorporating these practices, educators can empower students to develop both resilience and a versatile approach to utilizing technology in their academic endeavors.

1. **Explicit Strategy Instruction**

   Teach students a repertoire of cognitive strategies (e.g., summarizing, visualizing, questioning) and scaffold opportunities to apply them with digital tools. This builds both strategic flexibility and confidence. Refer back to Chapter 6 for more scaffolding ideas related to the habit of persistence.

2. **Student Goal-Setting and Reflection**

   Use tools like digital journals, goal trackers, or self-assessment checklists that prompt students to set learning intentions and reflect on the strategies they use. This not only promotes metacognition but reinforces the connection between effort and outcome—key to developing resilience (Yeager & Dweck, 2020).

3. **Tech-Integrated Problem-Solving**

   Incorporate tasks that require students to solve real-world problems using a variety of tools and approaches. Allow them to choose from a "menu" of digital resources (e.g., data analysis platforms, design software, research tools) and explain why they made those choices. This builds meta-strategic awareness of the tools at their disposal.

4. **Productive Struggle and Feedback Loops**

   Normalize trial and error. Create conditions where mistakes are expected, and feedback is framed around process: "What did you try?" "What did you learn from that approach?" "What strategy might work better next time?" These questions build a mindset of growth and adaptability.

5. **Collaborative Tech-Rich Projects**

   Encourage students to work in teams using digital tools to create, revise, and present work. Collaboration enhances resilience by requiring negotiation and adaptation, and it allows students to observe and learn from each other's strategic choices.

Equipping students to be both resilient and strategic learners means going beyond surface-level engagement with content or tools. It involves creating environments where students are aware of their thinking, are confident in their ability to navigate difficulty, and deliberate about how they use the tools and strategies at their disposal. By integrating technology in ways that invite reflection and strategy, teachers prepare students not just for academic success, but for a future where adaptability and thoughtful decision-making will be essential.

TEACHING TECH WITH INTENTION: SUPPORTING STUDENT WELL-BEING AND RESILIENCE

In our work with educators across varied contexts, one theme continues to emerge: students are overwhelmed. They're constantly toggling between tabs, devices, and distractions—often without the tools or guidance to manage it all in a way that feels healthy or purposeful. As educators, we have an opportunity—and responsibility—not just to integrate technology into learning, but to teach young people how to engage with it *intentionally*. We believe that helping students develop resilient learning habits must include helping them use technology in ways that promote well-being, agency, and long-term success.

In *Feel Good Productivity*, Ali Abdaal (2023) challenges the notion that productivity should feel pressured, fast-paced, or joyless. Instead, he argues that sustainable motivation grows from purpose, energy, and emotional alignment. We've seen the same to be true in resilient classrooms: when students are given the space and support to connect with *why* they're learning (just as you studied in Chapters 1 and 2 about beliefs and purpose) and *how* they feel while doing it, they're far more likely to remain engaged and confident—even when learning is hard.

Whether students realize it or not, their interactions with technology are emotional experiences. A messy desktop, a glitchy app, or an overflowing inbox can lead to frustration and disengagement. In contrast, a tool that's visually clear, easy to navigate, or that celebrates progress can spark motivation and joy. These small shifts matter. Abdaal reminds us that positive emotion is a driver of productivity—not a by-product. We would argue the same applies to learning.

When students use a task manager that allows them to check off goals and see their progress visually, or reflect on their learning in a digital journal, they're building both cognitive stamina and emotional confidence. These are the moments that feel good, and they reinforce a growth-oriented, resilient mindset.

FROM EFFICIENCY TO ALIGNMENT

Technology is often introduced in classrooms as a tool to streamline or enhance instruction—but what if we shifted the focus from efficiency to *alignment*? Instead of simply asking, "What tool should we use for this task?" we might ask, "How does this tool help students feel more in control of their learning?" or "Does this tech choice reduce friction and support student energy?"

Resilient students are not those who just "get through" a task—they're the ones who can name the strategy they chose, explain why they used it, and reflect on whether it helped. That's not just metacognition—it's meta-strategic thinking (Zohar & Barzilai, 2013). And it's something students can build through consistent, supported practice. When teachers model and scaffold intentional use of technology—naming how and why they use a specific platform, inviting students to choose tools that match their energy, or reflecting on what digital strategies felt most effective—they're helping students develop that same strategic awareness.

TEACHING HEALTHY DIGITAL BOUNDARIES

We cannot talk about resilience or student well-being without addressing the role of boundaries. Too often, students are given devices without any instruction in how to protect their attention, energy, or focus. And as educators, we've experienced how digital overload can chip away at our own capacity. That's why it's essential to teach students how to "pause before they click." A few practical strategies include:

- Starting lessons with an intention-setting moment: "What's our purpose for using this tool?"
- Modeling when and why to turn off notifications or exit distracting tabs, and
- Designing device-free transitions to support reflection or peer conversation.

These are not "extra" strategies. They are essential practices that nurture emotional regulation, clarity, and ownership—cornerstones of resilient learning.

Pause and Reflect

How might you intentionally model healthy digital boundaries for your students, and what routines could you introduce to help them build their own habits of focus and self-regulation?

____

____

____

In what ways could you embed device-free moments or reflective pauses in your lessons to strengthen students' ability to manage their attention and emotional energy?

____

____

____

TECHNOLOGY THAT BUILDS COMMUNITY AND CREATIVITY

At its best, technology should not isolate—it should connect. Tools that allow for collaboration as you examined in Chapter 3, or read-alouds and creative expression, for example, can build a sense of community and joy in the learning process. When students use multimedia platforms to co-create, peer-edit, or document their growth, they begin to see learning as *shared* and themselves as contributors to something bigger. In our work, we've seen that classrooms rooted in belonging and student agency are also the ones where students learn to use tech in ways that support, not replace, their humanity.

Helping students develop healthy tech habits is not about restricting use—it's about teaching them to *own* it. When technology use aligns with a student's sense of purpose and learning goals, it becomes a tool for resilience—not a threat to it.

STUDENT-FAMILY PARTNERSHIP REFLECTION

Navigating the intricate landscape of integrating technology into student learning pathways requires a collaborative student-family partnership approach. By acknowledging the challenges and strengths inherent in technology integration, these partnerships not only prioritize academic growth but also champion holistic development. Below are questions to help initiate these student-family partnership conversations when reflecting on the use of technology:

- In what ways does technology enhance or detract from your well-being and mental health?
- How do you maintain a healthy balance between using AI tools and fostering meaningful offline connections?
- What strategies can you implement to promote digital well-being and mindfulness while engaging with AI technologies in your learning journey?

The Big Ideas

In this chapter, we examined the transformative impact and challenges of technology on learners within the educational contexts. The seamless integration of artificial intelligence (AI) technologies has significantly elevated personalized learning experiences, offering students tailored support and resources aligned with their distinct educational needs. This strategic fusion has empowered students to excel academically, fostering an inclusive learning environment that caters to diverse learning styles and preferences. Furthermore, technology has expanded access to a wealth of educational resources and materials, breaking down geographical barriers and offering students a diverse range of perspectives to enrich their educational experiences. However, we reflected on the fact that amid these advancements, we underscored the importance of mitigating the risks of overreliance on technology, which could potentially undermine critical thinking and problem-solving skills essential for long-term academic and professional success. Furthermore, the ethical and privacy considerations tied to AI technologies call for meticulous scrutiny to ensure responsible and equitable deployment within educational settings, safeguarding student privacy and upholding ethical standards for a safe and inclusive learning atmosphere.

Let's Reflect

How can you leverage the expertise of key stakeholders, including students themselves, to collaboratively address the complexities of integrating technology into your instruction?

In what ways can you implement AI tools to promote academic integrity among students, ensuring that they grasp the importance of original work while utilizing technology to enhance their learning experiences?

How can you strike a balance between harnessing the benefits of technology in your classroom and minimizing excessive screen time for students, ensuring a balanced approach that supports their holistic development?

What's Next?

In Chapter 9, we will explore the integration of multiple modalities, including music, movement, and manipulatives, in the educational setting. This deliberate approach is crucial for nurturing resilient habits that encompass the entirety of a learner's being. Research underscores the profound impact of leveraging a variety of sensory experiences on cognitive development and the retention of information. Immersing students in music not only activates the auditory centers of the brain but also facilitates emotional regulation and aids in memory consolidation. Additionally, incorporating movement into educational practices has proven to boost concentration, foster creativity, and enhance overall academic performance. The strategic use of manipulatives has demonstrated the ability to stimulate spatial reasoning, refine fine motor skills, and sharpen problem-solving capabilities. By thoughtfully incorporating these multisensory strategies, educators can cultivate resilient behaviors that nurture comprehensive learning and bolster students' cognitive, emotional, and physical well-being.

CHAPTER 9

Harmonize Multimodal Learning

At the end of the quarter, Mia found herself slouched in her seat, disengaged as she toyed with her phone, while Taran, seated in the back row, showed clear signs of boredom by propping his feet on the desk and slipping in his earbuds. The traditional lecture-based approach from Mrs. Kekoa, filled with textbook problems, failed to capture their interest. The classroom environment, steeped in structure and repetition, no longer resonated with the post-pandemic reality of shortened attention spans and constant technology use. Recognizing the need for evolution in teaching methods, Mia and Taran's class longed for varied, interactive, and physically engaging learning experiences. The students needed a teacher to integrate multimodal strategies, blending technology, movement, creativity, and collaboration to reawaken curiosity and better align the learning experiences with their needs.

WHY MULTIMODAL LEARNING MATTERS

Both current and historic trends and research show that disengaged students are more likely to drop out of school. The National Center for Education Statistics (NCES, 2024) reported that in the school year 2021–2022 close to 900,000 high school students dropped out. "Factors such as lack of interest in classes, boredom, and disengagement from school contribute significantly to the decision to drop out" (Bridgeland et al., 2006). Facing these disheartening statistics, educators are compelled to consider classroom practices that invite students' engagement in their education. Strategies encompassed under the approach known as multimodal learning are not new, yet they offer a proven way of designing learning experiences that offer an entry point to addressing this widespread pattern of student disengagement.

Multimodal teaching is an instructional approach that engages multiple senses—visual, auditory, and kinesthetic—to help students process, understand, and retain information more effectively. In the ever-evolving landscape of education, this concept transcends mere technological integration. It underpins the very essence of how humans comprehend and retain information. By examining the deeper layers of the science of learning, we uncover the intricate tapestry of cognitive processes that determine effective education methodologies. For example, when we integrate sensory modalities such as auditory, kinesthetic, and visual elements into learning experiences, we are able to tap into the brain's innate ability to process information more efficiently and engage multiple regions simultaneously. By presenting information through diverse channels, we stimulate different cognitive pathways, reinforcing learning and improving retention.

Multimodal learning is different from strategies previously made popular known as teaching to an individual students' learning styles. Research routinely disproves a singular focus on one learning style—visual or auditory, for example—as having an effect (Hattie, 2020). Rather, multimodal teaching acknowledges that individuals have varied learning approaches and preferences, and thus leverages a combination of elements to cater to diverse and evolving learning needs (Figure 9.1). By infusing visual aids, interactive or kinesthetic activities, audio resources, and hands-on experiences into all types of instruction, multimodal learning aims to create a comprehensive and immersive learning environment that engages a broad spectrum of learners. Contemporary learners are natively familiar with, and likely to enthusiastically embrace, technology tools and resources—a tremendous additional opportunity for further elevating multimodal experiences for students. When students experience a variety of modalities to truly synthesize, and deepen their knowledge of, academic content and critical thinking skills, they are simultaneously afforded opportunities to explore, reflect, and express in ways that they best synthesize and apply content.

FIGURE 9.1 • Characteristics of Multimodal Learning

MULTIMODAL LEARNING IS . . .	MULTIMODAL LEARNING IS NOT . . .
• Incorporating various teaching methods such as visual, auditory, kinesthetic, music, and interactive elements to engage students.	• Relying solely on traditional lecture-based teaching methods without incorporating diverse modalities.
• Creating a learning environment that accommodates different learning preferences and styles.	• Using a one-size-fits-all instructional approach that doesn't consider individual differences in learning.
• Enhancing information processing and retention by tapping into multiple sensory channels in the brain.	• Limiting learning to a single mode of presentation, such as only using written text or lecture-style instruction.
• Fostering active participation and deeper understanding of the material through interactive and engaging activities.	• Maintaining a passive learning environment where students are predominantly passive recipients of information.
• Adapting to the evolving needs of modern education and leveraging diverse tools and technologies to support learning.	• Stagnating in outdated instructional practices that do not align with the digital age or the varied needs of today's learners.

WHAT NEUROSCIENCE SAYS ABOUT THE BENEFITS OF MULTIMODAL LEARNING

Neuroscience research has proven that multimodal learning has the ability to enhance and engage the learning process for students of all ages. Incorporating multimodal approaches into pedagogy aligns with established learning theories like constructivism and cognitivism. For example, by prompting students to engage with content through various modalities, educators activate prior knowledge, promote connections, and enhance understanding. This mirrors John Holt's (1983) view that learning is driven by the learner's activity, and John Dewey's (1893) philosophy that education is life itself. Scientific findings, such as those by Eric Jensen (2000), support the importance of physical movement in teaching and learning cycles for enhancing cognition and brain function. Multimodal strategies harmonize with these concepts

CONNECTION

Fostering multimodal learning naturally supports the habit of collaboration in Chapter 3 by equipping students with diverse ways to access, process, and share information, which enhances their ability to contribute meaningfully to group tasks and collective problem-solving.

and offer students immersive learning experiences reflecting the contemporary environment outside of the classroom. In essence, integrating multimodal learning practices in the classroom not only aligns with the science of learning but also empowers students to experience dynamic, engaging, and effective learning environments. By embracing the complexity of cognitive processes and leveraging different modalities, we unlock the full potential, in a holistic way, of students' intellectual growth, paving the way for educational experiences rooted in evidence-based practices and tailored to the intricate workings of the human mind.

WHERE TO BEGIN: ENGAGE STUDENTS IN A LEARNING STYLE REFLECTION

A multimodal reflection tool can help resilient learners identify and articulate ways that they prefer to engage in their learning and can promote self-awareness of their unique learning process. This reflection tool (see Figure 9.2) empowers learners to reflect, identify their preferred modes of engagement, and leverage a variety of modalities to enhance their academic experiences. First, determine students' level of need for support or scaffolding to engage in the reflection template. Facilitate the experience by reading the modalities, descriptions, and impacts as a group, for example, or independently if appropriate. Provide students the time to reflect on their personal confidence and/or preference for each modality using the column on the right to identify how significantly the respective modality impacts their engagement in learning.

This Student Engagement Modality Reflection Tool could also take various forms to more effectively achieve its purpose based on the age of the student.

- **Questionnaire:** A set of carefully crafted questions that explore students' beliefs about the impact of disengagement/engagement on their motivation
- **Journal prompt:** A series of prompts that encourage students to reflect on their learning and preferred or engaging learning styles
- **Class discussion:** Facilitated discussions where students share their preferred learning modality and how the collective learning environment can support them and the student support peers

FIGURE 9.2 ● Student Engagement Modality Reflection Tool

MODALITIES OF ACADEMIC ENGAGEMENT	DESCRIPTION/ EXAMPLE	IMPACT ON LEARNING	SCALE OF IMPACT AND REFLECTION (1–4 SCORE WITH 4 BEING THE HIGHEST)
Visual	Engaging with diagrams, creating or observing art, digital infographics charts, and educational videos to enhance understanding.	Visual representations aid in comprehension and retention of complex concepts with or without the use of multimedia.	*Example:* ***Score:*** *4* ***Reflection:*** *I know when I am able to use digital infographics, I remember both the process of how to do a task and the content better.*
Auditory	Participating in discussions, listening to or playing music, podcasts, audiobooks, and interactive audio resources.	Engaging through auditory channels enhances information processing and knowledge integration, through auditory processing and verbal expression.	Score: Reflection:
Kinesthetic	Hands-on activities, role-playing scenarios, virtual simulations, interactive labs, and using manipulatives.	Physical engagement supports experiential learning and memory retention through tactile experiences.	Score: Reflection:
Reading and Writing	Filling out notecatchers, utilizing e-books and digital research databases and collaborative online writing platforms or discussions.	Reading and writing activities promote literacy skills, critical analysis, and synthesis of knowledge.	Score: Reflection:
Reflective	Engage with digital reflection journals, self-assessment apps, and online portfolios. Contemplate learning experiences with peers in person and online as well as independently.	Reflection enhances metacognitive awareness and fosters deeper insights into personal learning styles and growth areas.	Score: Reflection:

Regardless of how the reflection tool is administered, helping students understand their preferred modalities of academic engagement can help them optimize their learning strategies, leverage their strengths, and expand their learning repertoire for enhanced academic success.

FROM THE LENS OF A STUDENT

Alexa's Engagement in Multimodal Instruction

In a bustling classroom, Alexa, a struggling high school student, was considering dropping out of school because she was not engaged and not feeling successful with her educational experience. Fortunately Alexa encountered a new teacher that provided a multitude of learning opportunities tailored to various modalities. With a knack for visual learning, Alexa thrived during interactive multimedia presentations that brought complex concepts to life. The integration of visual aids, such as infographics and educational videos, allowed Alexa to grasp and retain information more effectively, elevating her academic performance and confidence. Furthermore, the inclusion of hands-on activities and kinesthetic learning experiences provided a dynamic dimension to her education, enabling Alexa to engage deeply and apply theoretical knowledge in real-world contexts. This holistic approach to instruction not only fostered Alexa's academic growth but also supported a sense of belonging and appreciation for a variety of learning styles within the classroom environment. As a result, Alexa emerged as a well-rounded and confident learner, equipped with diverse learning experiences that catered to her individual strengths. This holistic approach not only empowered Alexa to excel academically but also instilled a deep sense of appreciation for the value of belonging and helped her to decide to continue on in her high school education.

APPLYING MULTIMODAL LEARNING STRATEGIES IN THE CLASSROOM

It is essential for all learners to recognize they have several ways in which they engage their senses to enhance the learning experience. When students engage multiple sensory channels, they are able to process information more effectively and retain knowledge for longer periods of time. However, one thing we know as teachers is that great learning often takes great planning, and multimodal teaching is no exception. It's easy to feel like designing lessons that use multiple modalities will take extra time, energy, and even resources. Hands-on materials and manipulatives can add costs that aren't always covered, and figuring out how to integrate all of it into your daily routines can seem overwhelming. These challenges aren't new, but they are real, and they're important to consider as we move toward making multimodal learning the norm for all students.

At the same time, we can't overlook how powerful multimodal teaching can be for engagement, understanding, and resilience. The series of three charts that follow offer opportunities to think through ways to weave multiple modalities into learning for your students. Many of these strategies are already part of strong teaching practices, but by being intentional, we can help students see, hear, feel, and do their way into deeper understanding. Multimodal learning isn't just a trend—it's a habit that supports every learner in building confidence and staying engaged.

Using Figure 9.3, read about each strategy to infuse multiple visual learning modalities into students' academic learning experiences. Then, reflect on how each strategy may enhance learning in your classroom and what first steps you might take to implement this modality.

Next, in Figure 9.4, read about each strategy to infuse multiple auditory modalities into students' academic learning experiences. Just as with the prior chart, reflect on how each strategy may enhance learning in your classroom and what first steps you might take to implement this modality.

Finally, carefully study each strategy for integrating various kinesthetic modalities into students' academic learning experiences, shown in Figure 9.5. Reflect on how each strategy may enhance learning in your classroom and what first steps you might take to implement this modality.

FIGURE 9.3 ● Enhancing Learning Through Visual Modalities Chart

VISUAL MODALITY STRATEGY	BENEFITS	REFLECTION: HOW MIGHT THIS STRATEGY ENHANCE LEARNING IN MY CLASSROOM?	REFLECTION: WHAT FIRST STEP COULD I TAKE TO TRY THIS STRATEGY?
Mental Models or Mind Maps: Utilize mind mapping tools to visually organize information and make connections between concepts.	Enhances critical thinking, promotes knowledge retention, and aids in creating a structured overview of complex topics.		
Infographics: Create or explore infographics to visualize data, processes, or content in a concise and engaging manner.	Facilitates easier understanding of complex information, improves information recall, and enhances visual appeal in presenting data.		
Concept Mapping: Utilize concept mapping software to visually depict the interconnectedness of ideas, terms, and theories.	Promotes a more profound grasp of the relationships among concepts, nurtures creativity in learning, and encourages critical analytical thinking.		
Visual Timelines: Construct visual timelines to chronologically represent historical events, developmental milestones, or project deadlines.	Fosters a deep understanding of chronological relationships, assists in retaining sequences of events, and offers a lucid portrayal of temporal connections.		
Digital Storytelling: Utilize digital storytelling by incorporating imagery, videos, and multimedia tools to effectively communicate narratives and concepts in a visually compelling manner.	Promotes creativity, enhances communication proficiency, and nurtures emotional engagement with educational content through the power of storytelling elements.		

FIGURE 9.4 • Enhancing Learning Through Auditory Learning Modalities Chart

AUDITORY MODALITY STRATEGY	BENEFITS	REFLECTION: HOW MIGHT THIS STRATEGY ENHANCE LEARNING IN MY CLASSROOM?	REFLECTION: WHAT FIRST STEP COULD I TAKE TO TRY THIS STRATEGY?
Podcasts: A digital audio program available for streaming or download, typically in episodic series, covering a wide range of topics from education and professional development to entertainment and current affairs.	Enriches the learning environment, offering versatile and accessible content.		
Audiobooks: Leverage digital audiobooks and e-readers as versatile tools to reinforce learning and comprehension conveniently.	With the aid of text-to-speech technologies and synchronized reading features, educators can seamlessly transition between auditory and visual modalities, catering to different sensory systems, which will increase the depth of knowledge.		
Music: Harness the potential of digital music streaming services and mnemonic aids powered by artificial intelligence to curate personalized soundscapes.	Integrates ambient background music and adaptive cognitive enhancement tools to optimize memory retention and cognitive performance, creating an environment conducive to focused learning and information absorption.		
Discussion: Leverage peer-to-peer conversations in class or video conferencing and discussion forums to facilitate insightful group discussions.	Promotes in knowledge-sharing, problem-solving, and information synthesis. Online forums provide a digital space for collaborative understanding and exchange of diverse perspectives, irrespective of geographical barriers.		

FIGURE 9.5 • Enhancing Learning Through Kinesthetic Learning Modalities Chart

KINESTHETIC MODALITY STRATEGY	BENEFITS	REFLECTION: HOW MIGHT THIS STRATEGY ENHANCE LEARNING IN MY CLASSROOM?	REFLECTION: WHAT FIRST STEP COULD I TAKE TO TRY THIS STRATEGY?
Hands-on Activities: Utilize manipulatives, experiments, and simulations.	Enhances tactile learning experiences, which increases engagement, retention, and understanding of abstract concepts.		
Mindful Movement Breaks: Incorporate short movement sessions between learning tasks.	Re-energizes and refocuses learners; increases heart rate and oxygen to the brain.		
Gesture-Based Learning: Encourage learners to use gestures and body movements, especially with academic language.	Reinforces memory and enhances comprehension.		
Combine physical activity with meaningful conversations. Students are given a prompt and walk around the room or a specified area to discuss the topic.	Stimulates creativity, promotes holistic well-being, fosters engagement, and inspires insightful discussions.		

Pause and Reflect

Which of the strategies from the visual, auditory, and kinesthetic tables feel most natural to incorporate into your current instructional practices, and why?

____

____

____

How might integrating multiple modalities into a single lesson support students with different learning preferences and strengthen their engagement and retention?

What small changes could you make to your daily routines or lesson design to intentionally weave in multimodal strategies that build students' confidence and resilience as learners?

By thoughtfully incorporating multimodal strategies such as these, among others, into daily practice, teachers can create learning environments where every student has an entry point to engage, process, and thrive. While the work requires intentional planning and collaboration, the payoff is a classroom filled with learners who feel confident, resilient, and connected to their growth.

FROM THE LENS OF A TEACHER

Mrs. Chun's Journey Through Multimodal Instruction

Mrs. Chun eagerly began planning an upcoming module on the solar system, excited to explore ways to make learning more engaging. The integration of multiple modalities quickly revealed itself as both a meaningful challenge and a rewarding opportunity. As she reviewed a wide range of resources to support diverse learners, she discovered creative ways to fine-tune her pedagogical approaches and incorporate strategies that met students where they were. Mrs. Chun's proactive mindset shone as she navigated the planning process, envisioning lessons where student engagement and comprehension would thrive in dynamic, multisensory ways.

(Continued)

(Continued)

She identified specific opportunities to embed visual supports like concept maps and infographics, auditory elements such as podcasts and music, and kinesthetic activities like hands-on models and movement-based discussions. Rather than feeling overwhelmed by time constraints, curriculum alignment, and the fast pace of educational technologies, Mrs. Chun reframed these factors as catalysts for innovation. With each new idea, she saw how these multimodal strategies could amplify students' curiosity and confidence, enabling them to interact with content more deeply. Her creative thinking, coupled with her resilience and dedication, reinforced her commitment to shaping learning environments where all students could flourish and build the habits of resilient, engaged learners.

PLANNING MULTIMODAL INSTRUCTION WITH MUSIC

One of the simplest and most powerful ways to increase student engagement through multimodal learning is by weaving music into the school day. You don't have to be a musician—you only have to be willing to let music support your students' learning. Research shows music activates multiple regions of the brain, boosting memory, attention, and even emotional regulation. As Kells (2008) notes, "Music has been shown to have a positive impact on literacy development . . . incorporating music into language and literacy activities can enhance various aspects of literacy skills" (p. 2). For younger learners, songs paired with clapping or rhythm sticks can make phonics or syllable work more memorable. Tapping beats while singing engages multiple senses at once, strengthening connections and improving focus. Practicing math facts with chants or songs also builds the fluency needed for tackling harder problems later on. Even in secondary classrooms, music supports learning. Background music during independent work promotes calm and focus. Setting science concepts, historical events, or vocabulary to tunes helps students recall content with ease.

As Jensen (2000) explains, "Music . . . engages emotions and enhances cognitive functions" (p. 117). Thoughtful integration of music turns lessons into multisensory experiences that deepen understanding and make learning stick. Review Figure 9.6 for the simple, practical strategies to incorporate music within your classroom that do not require extensive time or revising lesson plans!

FIGURE 9.6 ● Integrating Music in the Classroom

PURPOSE	SONG SUGGESTIONS
Fostering a Learning Environment: Play instrumental music softly in the background during individual work time, group activities, or transitions to create a conducive learning environment without overpowering instruction.	"Weightless," Marconi Union "Claire de Lune," Claude Debussy "Morning Mood," Edvard Grieg *Documentary Nature and Landscape*
Transitions: Use upbeat music during transitions between activities to signal time changes and help students shift their focus smoothly from one task to another.	"I Like to Move It," from the film *Madagascar* "Walking on Sunshine," Katrina and the Waves "Don't Stop Believin'," Journey "Here Comes the Sun," Beatles "Brave," Sara Bareilles "Lean on Me," Bill Withers "We Are Family," Sister Sledge "We're All in This Together," High School Musical Cast "You've Got a Friend in Me," Randy Newman
Learning and Memory: Integrate music with educational content by creating songs or chants to help students memorize facts, concepts, or procedures in a fun and engaging way.	Song suggestions: "Phonemic Awareness and Number Concepts," Dr. Jean Feldman "Learning Letter Sounds," Jack Hartmann "The Number Rock," Greg and Steve Classical options: "Cello Suite No. 1 in G Major," Bach, performed by Yo Yo Ma "The Four Seasons," Antonio Vivaldi
Enhanced Focus and Productivity: Music can aid in improving concentration, reducing distractions, and enhancing memory retention during tasks that require sustained attention.	Song suggestions: "Time," Hans Zimmer "Clarity," Ludovico Einaudi "Morning Mood," Edvard Grieg "Moonlight Sonata," Ludwig van Beethoven

(Continued)

(Continued)

PURPOSE	SONG SUGGESTIONS
Mood Regulation: Soothing melodies can be played to create a serene atmosphere perfect for mindfulness and stress relief, nurturing emotional well-being. Alternatively, play energetic, upbeat melodies to create a livelier atmosphere when scholars seem to be tired and need to be stimulated.	Song suggestions: "Somewhere Over the Rainbow," Harold Arlen & Yip Harburg, sung by Israel Kamakawiwo'ole "Lean on Me," Bill Withers "Can't Stop the Feeling," Justin Timberlake "What a Wonderful World," Bob Thiele & George David Weiss, sung by Louis Armstrong "Count on Me," Bruno Mars

By infusing enriching melodies and harmonies of your own selected instrumental pieces, you can orchestrate a symphony of productivity, creativity, and purpose for your learners, promoting the habit of multimodal learning.

LEVERAGING TECHNOLOGY TO ENHANCE MULTIMODAL LEARNING

Multimodal learning invites students to use multiple senses—visual, auditory, and kinesthetic—to process and retain information more deeply. Technology tools naturally align with this approach by offering varied ways for students to see, hear, and interact with academic content. Research supports this integration. Hattie (2020) highlights that when technology is used purposefully and blended with strong pedagogy, it can significantly boost student engagement and achievement.

For today's learners, technology isn't an add-on; rather, it's a language they speak fluently. Tablets, laptops, and even smartphones hold enormous potential for teachers seeking to create rich, multimodal learning environments. A digital whiteboard transforms lectures into interactive experiences where students can annotate, draw, or move elements to demonstrate understanding. Podcasts and audiobooks allow auditory learners to process content while strengthening listening skills, and virtual simulations engage kinesthetic learners in hands-on problem-solving without leaving the classroom.

Consider a fourth-grade teacher introducing fractions. Instead of relying on static worksheets, she uses an app where students manipulate virtual fraction bars, watch short explainer videos, and record themselves explaining their reasoning. This approach taps into multiple sensory channels and keeps students engaged because they can visualize, hear, and physically interact with the concepts. In high school, students might analyze primary sources using an online archive, create digital storyboards with images and text to map out historical events, and then present their findings in a video format. Here, technology enables students to approach the same content from different angles—building deeper understanding and practicing adaptability. This purposeful use of technology isn't just about novelty. It's about giving students opportunities to problem-solve, experiment, and reflect in ways that help them build resilience. When students troubleshoot a coding error, revise a multimedia presentation after peer feedback, or collaborate on a shared document, they're developing perseverance and flexibility—key qualities of resilient learners.

Moreover, tech-fueled multimodal learning gives students voice and choice. They can select tools and methods that align with their strengths or challenge them to grow in new ways. This sense of agency motivates learners and reinforces the belief that they are capable of navigating complexity and change.

When we intentionally pair technology with multimodal strategies, we don't just engage students in the moment. We help them develop the confidence, adaptability, and creative problem-solving skills they'll need long after they leave our classrooms.

MULTIMODAL LEARNING CULTIVATES RESILIENT LEARNERS

Multimodal learning helps students grow into confident, adaptable learners ready to take on complex challenges. Resilient learners are not defined by their ability to avoid difficulty but by their capacity to engage with it, learn from it, and emerge stronger. By engaging students through multiple modalities—visual, auditory, kinesthetic, and digital—we create layered learning experiences that allow them to build these critical skills.

When teachers model and guide students in using a variety of modalities purposefully, including digital tools, they nurture habits of resilience. For example, when students use technology to access visual supports, listen to a podcast for deeper context, and then work hands-on with peers to apply their learning, they're doing more than mastering content—they're practicing flexibility, collaboration, and problem-solving. These are the very skills they'll need in a rapidly changing world.

Resilient learners are also reflective. Multimodal strategies naturally encourage reflection because they ask students to consider: How do I learn best? What tools help me make sense of this concept? What strategies can I try if one approach doesn't work? This mindset shift—from passive recipient of information to active participant in learning—strengthens students' sense of agency. They begin to understand that setbacks are part of the process and that trying different approaches is a strength, not a failure.

Students gain valuable transferable skills along the way. For instance, creating multimedia projects develops critical thinking, creativity, and communication skills. Analyzing data in spreadsheets enhances logical reasoning and attention to detail. Collaborating in online spaces teaches digital citizenship and interpersonal skills in a digital context. These experiences prepare students for the demands of college, careers, and civic life. But even more importantly, they help students internalize the belief that they are capable of learning, adapting, and succeeding in new and unfamiliar situations.

Consider a middle school science class where students explore environmental issues. Some students create infographics using Canva to present their findings visually. Others record podcasts discussing their perspectives on conservation efforts. A few design hands-on models of ecosystems and film short explanatory videos to share with the class. This variety doesn't just cater to their learning preferences; it also pushes each student to engage creatively, use critical thinking, and collaborate with others. They are learning content while practicing resilience: adjusting to new tools, solving problems when technology doesn't work as planned, and seeing projects through to completion.

As educators, our goal isn't to make students experts in any one modality or tool, but to help them become agile learners who can access, process, and communicate information in multiple ways. Resilient learners aren't afraid to try, to fail, or to iterate. They understand that learning is dynamic and that they have the capacity to shape their own success. By fostering multimodal learning environments, we give students more than knowledge; we give them the tools and mindset to thrive in a world that will continue to demand adaptability, creativity, and perseverance.

STUDENT-FAMILY PARTNERSHIP REFLECTION

Incorporating multimodal learning strategies helps students engage with content in ways that align with their unique strengths and preferences, extending their opportunities for success beyond the classroom. To foster an authentic partnership with students and families, encourage these reflective questions at home to deepen a shared understanding of the child's learning journey:

- Which ways of learning—reading, listening, hands-on activities, or visual tools—help you understand new ideas best?
- How do you feel when you can use different ways to show what you know?
- What kinds of activities or tools make learning feel more fun or meaningful for you?
- How could we explore some of these strategies at home to help you with schoolwork?

When appropriate, invite families and students to share their reflections, creating a continuous cycle of engagement and growth.

The Big Ideas

In this chapter, we explored the powerful move of integrating multiple learning modalities to support resilient learners. Experiences that incorporate music, movement, and manipulatives play a vital role in fostering holistic development. Research consistently highlights the cognitive benefits of engaging the senses during learning—strengthening both understanding and retention. For example, musical activities not only activate the brain's auditory centers but also help regulate emotions and support memory. Movement has been shown to boost concentration, spark creativity, and improve academic outcomes. Similarly, the use of manipulatives, such as counters, blocks, and beads, enhances spatial reasoning, fine motor coordination, and problem-solving skills. By adopting and integrating these multisensory approaches, educators can effectively cultivate resilient habits that support comprehensive learning and enhance students' cognitive, emotional, and physical well-being.

Let's Reflect

How might you intentionally design learning experiences that integrate multiple modalities to support diverse learners in accessing and engaging with content?

____

____

____

In what ways could you identify and remove barriers that prevent students from fully benefiting from multimodal approaches, while building on strategies that are already working?

____

____

____

How do you know when your students are thriving with multimodal learning, and what evidence might you see that reflects growth in their confidence and learning outcomes?

____

____

____

What's Next?

In Chapter 10, you will learn about creating positive and comprehensive classroom culture and how it is paramount for fostering a conducive learning environment that develops resilient learners. Research has consistently shown that trust, hope, cultural consciousness, collective efficacy, and equity play important roles in shaping the overall educational experience. As we move forward to the final chapter, you will see how establishing trust between educators and scholars cultivates an environment where learners feel safe to take risks, ask questions, and engage in meaningful discussions, which leads us to our purpose in developing resilient learners.

CHAPTER 10

Cultivate Resilient Learning Habits

Every day in ninth-grade science felt heavier than the last for Jada. The equations, the lab write-ups, the constant rush of information—she could barely keep her head above water. Most mornings, she walked into class with her hoodie up, eyes down, just hoping not to get called on. She used to like science in middle school, but now, it all felt like too much. When her teacher, Mr. Nolan, passed back another quiz with a low grade scrawled in red ink, Jada barely looked at it before shoving it into her backpack. "I'm just not cut out for this," she muttered to herself. At the end of class, Mr. Nolan caught up with her. "I can see you're tired, Jada," he said gently. "But you're not alone. Every great scientist started out by getting things wrong. What matters is showing up and learning from it." She looked at him, surprised by the lack of disappointment in his voice. He wasn't judging—he was encouraging. That night, for the first time in weeks, Jada opened her notebook at home. She wasn't sure where to start, but something Mr. Nolan said stuck: "Resilience isn't about never struggling. It's about learning to move forward anyway."

WHY RESILIENCE MATTERS

Throughout your journey reading about the habits for resilient learners, you have developed a rich portfolio of both instructional and relational practices that lead toward this ultimate goal: developing young people capable of thriving no matter what environment in which they find themselves. Connecting each of the habits within and throughout the school days and across the years will collectively serve to embed the principles and mindsets described here in the final habit, cultivating resilience. Fundamental to your success, however, is aligning your understanding of resilience to research and discerning fact from popular myths that pervade society. As described in our book *Habits of Resilient Educators* (Prendergast & Lee, 2024), the proven factors that contribute to resilience in your students are no different than those in yourself or the adults around you. Beyond the notion that resilience simply implies someone who grits their teeth (metaphorically) and learns to endure trauma, tragedy, and other obstacles, resilience is in fact a way of thinking that is grounded in these factors that may be proactively developed. Southwick and Charney (2018) define them as the following:

1. Realistic optimism
2. Facing fear
3. Moral compass
4. Religion or spirituality
5. Social support
6. Resilient role models
7. Physical fitness
8. Brain fitness
9. Cognitive and emotional flexibility
10. Meaning and purpose

You may notice aspects of these ten factors that have been described within the habits thus far or draw connections to other areas of your expertise and personal experience. For the young people in our classrooms, each of these habits is intentionally connected to enabling you to support and nurture lifelong resilience alongside them. In this final chapter, you'll examine even more detail around key practices for achieving this goal and, ultimately, enhance your students' overall well-being and experiences of belonging in school (Figure 10.1).

FIGURE 10.1 • Characteristics of Resilient Learning Habits

RESILIENT LEARNING HABITS ARE . . .	RESILIENT LEARNING HABITS ARE NOT . . .
• Developed through consistent practice and reflection over time.	• Instinctive traits students are either born with or without.
• Supported by clear routines that promote self-awareness and goal-setting.	• Built solely through praise or encouragement without explicit instruction.
• Strengthened when students are taught how to respond constructively to setbacks.	• The same as perfectionism, compliance, or passive endurance.
• Connected to real-world purpose, identity, and meaningful learning experiences.	• Developed in isolation from social-emotional and academic contexts.

RESILIENT LEARNING HABITS IN AN ERA OF V.U.C.A.

Just as teaching has shifted into a profession marked by constant change, our students are learning in a world defined by volatility, uncertainty, complexity, and ambiguity—what researchers refer to as the V.U.C.A. era. Originally used to describe the post–Cold War military landscape (Bennett & Lemoine, 2014), the term now feels fitting for daily life in schools. Whether it's adapting to evolving technologies, navigating social unrest, or facing the ripple effects of a pandemic that disrupted learning for an entire generation, today's students are growing up in conditions where the only constant is uncertainty.

In this climate, resilience is not a luxury—it's a necessity. We're not talking about grit as a buzzword or blind perseverance. We're talking about a grounded, teachable set of habits that help students respond to setbacks with reflection, purpose, and flexibility. Habits like setting meaningful goals, talking to themselves with compassion, embracing feedback, and asking questions that drive deeper learning. These are not quick fixes, but they are manageable, sustainable practices that build both academic strength and personal capacity. When students begin to internalize these routines, they don't just survive school—they start to thrive in spite of its challenges.

And here's the part that matters for you: cultivating resilience doesn't require you to overhaul your teaching or add more to your already overflowing plate. Instead, it invites you to embed what matters most into what you already do. Goal-setting becomes part of morning meetings. Reflection can be integrated into exit slips. Collaborative norms may be strengthened in group work. When resilience is woven into the fabric of daily instruction, you support student growth in a way that enhances—not competes with—your academic goals. Resilience isn't the cure for every challenge in education, but it's a practical, human-centered approach that meets this moment with clarity and hope.

RESILIENCE AND STUDENT ENGAGEMENT: AN INHERENT CONNECTION

Across the globe, troubling data reveal that more and more students are disconnecting from school. Chronic absenteeism rates have surged in the wake of the COVID-19 pandemic, with over one in four students in the United States missing 10 percent or more of the school year—an alarming indicator of widespread disengagement (U.S. Department of Education, 2023). This isn't just about attendance; it reflects deeper feelings of disconnection, lack of purpose, and diminished belief in the value of schooling. For educators, this reality underscores an urgent question: how do we reengage students not just in school but in learning itself?

The answer lies in cultivating resilient learning habits—habits that help students find meaning, navigate challenge, and develop the skills needed to persist in uncertain environments. When students are equipped with tools like goal-setting, emotional regulation, self-reflection, and cognitive flexibility, they are far more likely to feel capable, connected, and invested in their learning. Resilience is not a side benefit of education—it is a prerequisite for student engagement. When students believe they can overcome setbacks, when they see growth as possible and learning as purposeful, they show up differently. They begin to reengage, not because they're told to but because they're internally motivated to.

At the heart of strong instruction is student intellectual engagement—the kind of thinking that asks students to analyze, question, create, and connect. But intellectual engagement doesn't happen through worksheets or compliance. It happens when students are doing the thinking—not just the task. When we foster resilience in learning, we prepare students to stay with a problem even when it's hard, to rethink an idea even when it's unfamiliar, and to reflect on their process with growing independence. These skills foster ownership, which in turn deepens engagement.

Educators can cultivate these habits by embedding metacognitive routines, reflective questioning, and moments of productive struggle into daily instruction. Asking students to revisit an error, explain their reasoning, or revise their work not only builds academic skill—it teaches them to persist through uncertainty. When we normalize struggle and explicitly teach the habits that support perseverance, we change the emotional experience of learning. And while this may feel like one more thing in an already overwhelming profession, it's not. Building resilience doesn't require a new curriculum or more instructional time—it requires being intentional about the habits we model, reinforce, and prioritize.

Resilience bridges the gap between academic rigor and emotional well-being. It helps students show up more fully—not just in attendance, but in presence, effort, and belief. And in this moment—when student engagement is more fragile than ever—it is one of the most urgent and impactful things we can teach. In *Reimagining Student Engagement: From Disrupting to Driving*, Amy Berry (2022) highlights that authentic engagement occurs when students move from passive compliance to actively driving their own learning. Figure 10.2 illustrates six forms of student engagement in planned learning experiences ranging from active disengagement to active engagement.

FIGURE 10.2 • Disrupting to Driving: A Continuum of Student Engagement

ACTIVE ◄——— PASSIVE ———► ACTIVE

	DISRUPTING	AVOIDING	WITHDRAWING	PARTICIPATING	INVESTING	DRIVING
Engaging in the activity	Disrupting the learning environment Refusing to participate Arguing with the teacher	Looking for ways to avoid work Being off-task Being unprepared Looking for reasons to leave the room or move around the room	"Flying under the radar" Physically separating from others Being distracted Putting in low effort	Doing the work Being on-task Paying attention Responding to questions	Asking questions about what we are learning Valuing what we are learning Showing interest or curiosity in what we are learning Enjoying learning	Setting goals for my learning Seeking feedback to help me improve Seeking out challenges Monitoring and evaluating my progress
Engaging with peers	Arguing with peers Trying to distract others	Off-task talking with others Playing around with others instead of working	Sitting with a group if directed but not interacting	Working with others when directed to do so	Sharing ideas and thinking with peers Following shared interests	Collaborating with others toward a shared goal Challenging each other to drive improvement
	Students are disengaging from the planned learning experience			Students are engaging in the planned learning experience		
What goals might the teacher have for engagement in the learning experience?				I want them to follow my lead and complete certain tasks	I want them to be interested in learning and actively involved in the process	I want them to be proactive and collaborative learners

Berry, A. (2022). *Reimagining student engagement: From disrupting to driving*. Corwin.

Pause and Reflect

Now that you have explored Berry's continuum, consider the reflection questions below as you connect these concepts to your own understanding of engagement.

How do I currently define student engagement, and in what ways might I be confusing "on-task behavior" with true intellectual engagement?

When planning lessons, how often do I consider whether students will be doing the thinking—not just the work—and how might this shift my instructional design?

What routines or strategies could I use to help students reflect on their thinking (not just their answers), and how might this deepen both their learning and their resilience?

The *habits for resilient learners* directly support students to move through this continuum toward intellectual engagement by equipping them with the internal tools to stay curious, manage challenges, and take ownership of their growth. Together, each of the habits transforms engagement from something teachers *manage* to something students *embody*. In Figure 10.3, you will notice each of the habits listed on the left, with some examples completed for you of how each habit contributes to students' resilience as well as how the habit fosters engagement in their learning. Brainstorm your own ideas, or collaborate with colleagues, to complete the chart.

FIGURE 10.3 ● How Each Habit Contributes to Student Resilience and Engagement

HABIT NAME	CONTRIBUTES TO STUDENTS' RESILIENCE BY . . .	FOSTERS STUDENTS' ENGAGEMENT IN THEIR LEARNING BY . . .
Habit 1: Nurture Core Beliefs	Building students' self-efficacy and belief in their ability to grow, learn, and overcome setbacks.	
Habit 2: Clarify Student Success		Encouraging ownership by aligning learning to personally meaningful definitions of success.
Habit 3: Move From Groups to Team Collaboration	Strengthening interpersonal resilience through shared responsibility, communication, and trust-building.	
Habit 4: Empower Learners Through Goal-Setting	Developing agency and motivation by teaching students how to break challenges into manageable steps.	
Habit 5: Navigate the Feedback Process	Encouraging adaptability and growth mindset by normalizing critique and revision as learning tools.	
Habit 6: Persevere Through Obstacles		Building confidence and momentum as students experience success through struggle.
Habit 7: Embrace Vulnerability	Creating psychological safety, fostering resilience through openness and risk-taking in learning.	
Habit 8: Develop Tech-Savvy Scholars		Engaging students through relevant tools, expanding their ability to learn, create, and communicate.
Habit 9: Harmonize Multimodal Learning		Promoting sustained attention and enthusiasm through varied and student-centered learning experiences.

For students to thrive in today's uncertain world they need more than the ability to complete tasks—they need the confidence to approach challenges with curiosity and persistence. This requires teaching that goes beyond surface-level processing to foster deeper connections, reflection, and purpose. As shown in the previous chart, each habit strengthens both resilience and engagement: when students set goals, navigate feedback, collaborate effectively, and reflect on their thinking, they become more invested in learning and better equipped to handle difficulty. These outcomes are mutually reinforcing—resilient students engage more deeply, and engaged students grow more resilient. Rather than adding more to educators' workloads, this approach helps focus teaching on what matters most: developing capable, adaptive, lifelong learners.

FROM THE LENS OF A TEACHER

Ms. Hall Teaches Realistic Optimism

Ms. Hall had been teaching twelfth grade for over two decades, but this year felt different. Her seniors—usually buzzing with anticipation for graduation—were flat. Assignments went untouched, cameras stayed off during virtual office hours, and when she asked for reflections, she was met with blank stares or shrugged shoulders. "What's the point?" one student finally admitted. "It's not like anything's going to change for us." That sentence echoed in her mind for days. Ms. Hall knew what they were feeling wasn't laziness—it was exhaustion, a quiet grief for lost normalcy, and fear of the unknown. So she decided to shift gears. She scrapped a planned lecture and instead shared a story of one of her former students who had failed her final project but later built a career from the lessons she learned in that failure. Then, she introduced a new routine: "Resilience Check-Ins." Once a week, students wrote one challenge they faced and one thing—no matter how small—they could still control or look forward to. At first, the responses were sparse. But slowly, glimmers of hope appeared. "I can't fix everything at home, but I can finish this essay." Ms. Hall smiled. They weren't there yet, but they were learning realistic optimism—one step at a time.

CULTIVATING RESILIENT LEARNING HABITS WITH A MENTOR MINDSET

Another powerful way educators can nurture resilient learning habits is by embracing a *mentor mindset*, a way of teaching that centers on guidance, partnership, and student ownership. Drawing from David Yeager's *10 to 15: The Science of Motivating Young People* (2024), the mentor mindset moves educators beyond traditional roles of directing and correcting and toward practices that build student agency, engagement, and long-term motivation. Central to this shift is the understanding that resilience is not built by telling students what to do but by helping them discover how to think, reflect, and respond when learning gets hard.

ASK MORE, TELL LESS: BUILDING OWNERSHIP THROUGH QUESTIONS

One of the foundational strategies of the mentor mindset is asking more questions instead of always giving directions or solutions. For example, consider the power of reflective questioning in fostering ownership (Brueggeman, 2022). When teachers ask, "What strategy might work next?" or "How do you know this is the best evidence to support your claim?" they prompt learners to engage in metacognition, a resilient learning habit that strengthens both problem-solving and self-confidence.

Yeager (2024) reinforces this idea, noting that adolescents and young learners are most motivated when they feel respected and autonomous. Instead of interpreting student struggles as lack of effort, teachers who adopt a mentoring approach understand these moments as opportunities to ask thoughtful questions and guide students toward their own solutions. This shift not only helps students become more resilient thinkers but also strengthens the teacher-student relationship—a key driver of motivation. When students demonstrate the behavior of chronically submitting learning assignments well after class deadlines, for example, it's natural to develop the perception that they are lazy, disorganized, or apathetic. Adults are at risk for immediately applying a critical, punishing-oriented approach to "tell the student what they did wrong" or ensure they comply with our expectations in the future. At the root of this approach is likely a desire to encourage the student to take responsibility for, or to take ownership of, their behavior and ultimately the effect it has on their learning. By using Yeager's approach of questioning instead of telling, consider how this goal might instead be achieved if teacher and student (and parent, where appropriate) worked together to identify the root cause of the behavior.

FROM THE LENS OF A STUDENT

Daweet Begins to Understand Resilience

At the beginning of first grade, Daweet used to think he was just bad at a lot of things. If he couldn't read a word right away or if his drawing didn't look like his friend's, he'd crumple his paper and say, "I can't do this!" Sometimes, when his little brother messed with his toys, he'd scream or cry. Everything felt too hard. But then, in class, they started learning something called "bounce-back strategies." Daweet's teacher, Ms. Ray, told us that our brains could grow stronger just like muscles. They talked about taking deep breaths when they were upset, using kind words when they disagreed, and saying things like "I can't do this yet." At first, Daweet didn't believe it. But then one day, he messed up during our morning meeting, and instead of hiding, he took a deep breath and tried again. His friend smiled and said, "Good job!" Now, when he feels stuck or mad, he tries to remember what Ms. Ray says: "You're learning how to do hard things." He still gets frustrated sometimes, but he doesn't give up as fast. Daweet is even beginning to think he's becoming someone who keeps going—even when things are tricky. He reflects to himself, "I think that's what being resilient means."

PROMOTING POSITIVE SELF-TALK

Resilient learners are not just those who keep going—they are those who persist with *purpose*, guided by an internal belief that effort matters and that growth is possible. One of the most foundational, yet often overlooked, elements of building this resilience is nurturing students' inner dialogue. Self-talk—what students say to themselves in the privacy of their thoughts—can either fuel learning or silently undermine it. Many students, especially those who have experienced repeated setbacks, carry internal narratives shaped by shame or failure: "I'm not smart enough," "I never get this right," or "Why should I even try?" These beliefs often go unspoken, yet they have a powerful impact on motivation, confidence, and engagement.

As educators, we may not always hear these statements out loud, but we can see their effects. Students who rush through work or shut down during a challenge may be avoiding the discomfort of failure—not because they're unwilling to learn but because they've come to believe that success is beyond their reach. These narratives are not fixed. With intention and support, they can be rewritten. Promoting positive self-talk is not about forced optimism or cheerleading; it's about helping students develop a realistic and compassionate inner voice that supports learning rather than derails it.

Teachers can begin cultivating this shift by modeling powerful yet simple language changes in daily interactions. When a student struggles with a math problem and says, "I can't do this," the teacher might respond, "You can't do it *yet*. What's one strategy we've used before that you could try?" This subtle shift introduces the language of growth without ignoring the struggle. Another approach is asking students, "What would you say to a friend who felt this way?" This externalization helps students see their self-talk more objectively and often reveals how much more compassion they show to others than to themselves.

Yeager's research offers strong support for these practices. He explains that young people are most motivated when they see effort and persistence as part of who they are—not just something they're told to do. He calls this a "*purpose mindset*," the belief that learning is not just about short-term success but about becoming someone who can contribute meaningfully to the world. As you learned in Chapter 6, "Persevere Through Obstacles," when students view struggle as evidence that they're in the process of learning something important, rather than as proof of inadequacy, they are more likely to keep going. And over time, they begin to develop an identity grounded in resilience rather than avoidance.

Classroom routines can be powerful vehicles for this work. For example, goal-setting conferences like those you examined in Chapter 4 provide moments for students to reflect on how they've grown, where they've faced difficulty, and what they're proud of. Teachers can guide students to use affirming, realistic language in these reflections: "I struggled with this at first, but now I understand," or "Next time, I'll try a different approach." Peer feedback routines such as those you explored through Chapter 5 can also reinforce positive self-talk when structured intentionally. Instead of generic praise or criticism, students can be taught to offer feedback that is growth-oriented, specific, and encouraging—helping both giver and receiver build constructive inner dialogue.

Another effective strategy is creating classroom visuals or anchor charts of "resilient phrases." These could include "Mistakes help me learn," "I can try a new strategy," or "I'm not there yet, but I'm working on it." Referencing these phrases during instruction not only normalizes the language of persistence and makes it part of the classroom culture, it builds on the habits of nurturing core beliefs and cultivating purpose in Chapters 1 and 2. Over time, students begin to internalize these phrases, especially when they are consistently modeled by adults.

It's also essential to understand that promoting positive self-talk is not about denying real challenges. Students may be facing academic gaps, learning differences, or personal stressors that make learning hard. Acknowledging these realities while offering supportive strategies is key. For instance, rather than saying, "You'll be fine," a teacher might say, "This is a hard concept, and that's OK. Let's figure out what part is confusing and work through it together." This blend of empathy and problem-solving reinforces the idea that struggle is not a sign of failure—it's a natural part of growth.

Ultimately, helping students develop healthier self-talk is about giving them tools they can carry beyond the classroom. It strengthens both cognitive resilience—the ability to problem-solve and persist—and emotional resilience—the capacity to regulate discouragement and stay grounded in self-belief. As students begin to coach themselves through challenges, they become more confident, more engaged, and more empowered in their own learning journey. And that, more than any score or outcome, is what prepares them for the complexity of learning and life.

APPLYING THE SCIENCE OF PURPOSE

Mentoring is not just about improving performance—it's about developing the whole person (Brueggeman, 2022). When students understand their learning in the context of personal and social purpose, they are more likely to stick with it, even when it gets hard. As you learned in Chapter 1, "Nurturing Core Beliefs," we know that students are far more likely to be resilient when they see their learning as meaningful—not just for personal success but for contributing to something larger than themselves. This science of purpose underscores how critical it is for teachers to help students understand the "why" behind their learning experiences.

Teachers can apply this by helping students draw connections between content and real-world impact. For instance, in a science lesson, a teacher might ask, "How could this learning help you solve a problem in your community?" In writing, students might reflect on, "Who needs to hear your story or perspective, and why?" These questions anchor academic tasks in a sense of relevance and contribution, both of which fuel intrinsic motivation.

Figure 10.4 provides examples of purpose-based resilience activities to deepen the alignment of classroom learning experiences to the science of purpose, the habit of nurturing core beliefs, and the overall cultivation of resilient learning habits. In the table, identify activities you may have already implemented

FIGURE 10.4 • Purpose-Based Resilience Activities

ACTIVITY	I TRIED THIS BEFORE, AND THIS IS HOW IT WENT	THIS IS NEW TO ME, AND I WILL APPLY IT IN . . .
Start class with a "Resilience Question of the Day," like "What challenge did you overcome this week?" or "What's one strategy you've used to keep going when things got tough?"		
Use conferencing and check-ins to guide students with open-ended questions, like "What do you notice about your progress?" or "What's something you've learned about how you learn?"		
Model vulnerability by sharing your own learning struggles and how you pushed through them, reinforcing that resilience is a habit, not a fixed trait.		
Create space for student-led goal-setting and allow students to track and revise their goals regularly. Celebrate effort, not just outcomes.		
Integrate purpose-driven learning tasks by inviting students to connect what they're learning to issues that matter to them, their families, or their communities.		

and what outcomes you noticed, or, for those that are new, use the chart to identify in what setting you may implement the activity in the future.

When teachers adopt a mentor mindset, they foster a classroom environment where students are encouraged to think deeply, reflect honestly, and persist purposefully. As both Yeager and Brueggeman argue, motivation and growth don't emerge from control; rather, they emerge from connection, purpose, and trust. And when those elements are present, students don't just learn—they thrive.

STUDENT-FAMILY PARTNERSHIP REFLECTION

By now, you may be very familiar with this reflection opportunity from the other chapters. In this final chapter, consider how you can help families see the connections between resilience and all of the habits their child has been developing. When introducing this activity, remind families it is about having a supportive conversation—not giving advice or evaluating their child's answers. Encourage them to listen with curiosity, share their own stories of resilience, and celebrate small wins together.

1. Can you tell me about a time at school when something felt really hard? What helped you keep going or try again?
2. When you're stuck on a tough problem or project, what words do you say to yourself to stay positive? Do you think those words make a difference?
3. How have your teamwork, goal-setting, or feedback skills helped you bounce back from challenges this year?

By engaging families in their child's learning about resilience, you not only reinforce the habits students are developing but also create a shared language of growth and perseverance. Investing in these partnerships often leads to students showing greater confidence, deeper engagement, and a stronger sense of belonging in both their classroom and family life.

The Big Ideas

In this final chapter, you've seen how resilience is not built through a single moment of bravery but through a consistent system of habits practiced over time. Throughout the book, you explored ten habits that help learners thrive—not just in school but also in life. You reflected on how asking questions fosters curiosity, how handling stress builds coping strategies, and how students can learn to talk to themselves with self-compassion and clarity. You learned to recognize when resilient learning is taking root and how to support it. Most importantly, you've come to understand resilience as a mindset grounded in key elements like realistic optimism, facing fear, cognitive flexibility, and purpose. These principles, drawn from research by Southwick and Charney (2018), serve as the backbone for the habits you've developed alongside your students.

As you integrate these habits into your teaching, remember: your influence doesn't just shape academic skills—it builds identity, agency, and hope. When students practice resilience every day, they leave your classroom not only more capable but more confident in who they are and who they are becoming. That is the true impact of teaching with resilience in mind.

Let's Reflect

How might you intentionally structure daily learning experiences to support students in developing habits of reflection, self-talk, and adaptive problem-solving?

____

____

____

In what ways could you help students recognize the connection between challenge and growth, and guide them to interpret setbacks with realistic optimism and flexible thinking?

____

____

____

How do you know when your students are becoming more resilient learners, and what evidence might you see—through their questions, engagement, and self-assessment—that shows growth in their agency and sense of purpose?

____

____

____

What's Next?

You've reached the end of *Habits for Resilient Learners*, but your journey and that of your students is just beginning. The habits in these chapters are meant to be lived, revisited, and adapted over time. As you begin to apply the activities and strategies in your classroom or learning environment, return to the chapters that resonate most—or those that challenge you. Each time you do, you'll gain new insight, deepen your confidence, and discover more ways to nurture resilience in your students. Remember: resilience is not a fixed trait but a mindset and set of practices that grow with intention and reflection. Keep modeling curiosity, adaptability, and belief in your learners' potential. You are shaping the way students respond to challenges, relate to themselves and others, and carry forward a strong sense of agency.

Epilogue

Your learning doesn't stop here. If anything, this is where it begins—again.

With each chapter of *Habits for Resilient Learners*, you've explored a specific, research-based habit designed to cultivate confidence, curiosity, and capability in your students. But even more importantly, you've taken a journey that likely reconnected you to your own *why*—the purpose and passion that brought you to the classroom in the first place.

Each page was meant to affirm what you already know: teaching is a deeply human practice. It asks you to be flexible and consistent, thoughtful and responsive, hopeful and realistic—all at the same time. And it calls on you to model what resilience looks like, even when you're still building it yourself.

That's what makes this work so powerful.

As a teacher, you already have the tools to begin cultivating resilience in your learners—because you *are* a resilient learner. You reflect, you adapt, you persist. Now, you also have a framework to guide your next steps, with habits that can be taught, shared, and strengthened together in your classroom community.

WHY REFLECT NOW?

Reflection transforms information into intention. Before you turn the page on this experience, take a moment to notice how you've grown:

- What surprised you most about the habits?
- Which chapter felt like it was written *just for you*?
- What small strategy did you try—and what did you learn from that?
- Where do your students already show signs of resilience?
- Where are they asking (silently or out loud) for support?

These questions aren't rhetorical—they're relationship-building. They help you track what matters and set a direction that feels rooted in reality, not just aspiration.

And just like the habits we introduced, reflection is more powerful when practiced consistently and in community. Don't keep your learning to yourself. Talk about it. Journal about it. Share it with a colleague or a student. Collaborate on ways to keep the habits alive beyond this reading.

WHAT HAPPENS WHEN WE PRACTICE THESE HABITS TOGETHER?

Real change happens when these habits move beyond the page and into the patterns of a classroom. When students start defining success in their own words, the energy in the room changes. When they engage with feedback as a tool—not a threat—they show up differently. When learners embrace questions, set their own goals, and support each other like true teammates, they don't just *do school*—they start *owning* their learning.

You've now seen how each habit does more than address an academic skill—it develops a whole person:

- Self-awareness flourishes when core beliefs are nurtured.
- Agency emerges when students understand success and set aligned goals.
- Belonging is built when teams collaborate and shared vulnerability becomes normal.
- Persistence grows when challenges are expected, not feared.
- Confidence increases when feedback is seen as a path toward growth.

And for educators? These habits help you anchor your practice during uncertain times. They offer a structure for instructional decision-making, classroom management, and emotional presence. They strengthen student-teacher relationships. They reduce friction. And they return a sense of joy to the heart of teaching.

A FEW IDEAS TO CARRY THIS WORK FORWARD

No single approach works for every learner—or every teacher. But here are a few ways you might continue the momentum:

- Choose one habit each month to focus on as a team. Set goals. Try strategies. Debrief together.
- Involve students in the reflection process. What do *they* notice about their resilience?
- Build a habit tracker for your class. Let learners document their progress over time.
- Start a lunch-and-learn series with your colleagues to revisit key chapters or habits.
- Design your own professional learning using the book as a flexible framework.
- Reconnect with your accountability partner if you read this book in a pair or group. Set a date to reflect together.

These ideas are just starting points. There's no single "right way" to apply this content—only meaningful ways that align with your values, your context, and your students.

LET THIS BE AN ONGOING CONVERSATION

As authors, we wrote this book from classrooms, not ivory towers. We've been in your shoes. We've supported students who seemed unreachable, and we've doubted ourselves along the way. What kept us going—and still does—is the belief that resilience is *relational*. It grows best when it's nurtured by people who care. That includes you.

So if this book spoke to you, please pay it forward. Pass it on. Recommend a chapter. Facilitate a study group. Better yet, share your story. Let others know what happened when you introduced a habit in your classroom. Your insight might be the spark someone else needs to begin. Your journey as a builder of resilient learners is far from over. In fact—it's just beginning.

My Learning Intentions at the Conclusion of This Book Are . . .

1.
2.
3.

References

Abdaal, A. (2023). *Feel-good productivity: How to do more of what matters to you*. Celadon Books.

Almarode, J., Fisher, D., Thunder, K., & Frey, N. (2021). *The success criteria playbook: A hands-on guide to making learning visible and measurable*. Corwin.

Almarode, J., & Vandas, K. (2018). *Clarity for learning: Five essential practices that empower students and teachers*. Corwin.

American Psychological Association. (2020). *What the research shows: Multitasking*. Retrieved July 2025, from https://www.apa.org/topics/research/multitasking

Bandura, A. (1997). *Self-efficacy: The exercise of control*. Freeman.

Bennett, N., & Lemoine, G. J. (2014). What VUCA really means for you. *Harvard Business Review, 92*(1–2), 27.

Berry, A. (2022). *Reimagining student engagement: From disrupting to driving*. Corwin.

Bogiou, T. (2025, March). *2,500 years ago they knew* [Online forum post]. LinkedIn.

Bridgeland, J. M., DiIulio, J. J., Jr., & Morison, K. B. (2006). *The silent epidemic: Perspectives of high school dropouts*. A report by Civic Enterprises in association with Peter D. Hart for the Bill & Melinda Gates Foundation. https://docs.gatesfoundation.org/Documents/Thesilentepidemic3-06final.Pdf

Brown, B. (2012). *Daring greatly: How the courage to be vulnerable transforms the way we live, love, parent, and lead*. Gotham Books.

Brown, B. (2021). *Atlas of the heart: Mapping meaningful connection and the language of human experience*. Random House.

Brueggeman, A. (2022). *Student-centered mentoring: Keeping students at the heart of new teachers' learning*. Corwin.

Bruner, J. S. (1978). The role of dialogue in language acquisition. In A. Sinclair, R. J. Jarvella, & W. J. M. Levelt (Eds.), *The child's concept of language* (pp. 241–256). Springer.

Carrington, J. (2019). *Kids these days: A game plan for (re)connecting with those we teach, lead, & love*. FriesenPress.

CASEL. (n.d.). *What is the CASEL framework?* https://casel.org/fundamentals-of-sel/what-is-the-casel-framework/

CASEL. (2020). CASEL's SEL framework. https://casel.org/casel-sel-framework-11-2020/

Chappuis, J., & Stiggins, R. (2020). Classroom assessment for student learning (3rd ed.). Pearson.

Clark, J. (2025). Cognitive load theory: Six strategies to tailor instruction for maximum learning [Poster based on J. Sweller et al. (2017). *Cognitive load theory: Research that teachers really need to understand: Classroom practice guide*. Centre for Education Statistics and Evaluation]. https://www.jamieleeclark.com/graphics?trk=public_post_reshare-text

Couros, G. (2015). *The innovator's mindset: Empower learning, unleash talent, and lead a culture of creativity*. Dave Burgess Consulting.

Cullins, A. (n.d.). 7 Ways to instill a love of learning in children. *Big Life Journal*. https://biglifejournal.com/blogs/blog/instill-love-learning-children

Danielson, C., Furman, L., & Kappes, L. (2024). *Enhancing professional practice: The framework for teaching* (3rd ed.). ASCD.

Dewey, J. (1893). Self-realization as the moral ideal. *Philosophical Review, 2*(6), 652–664.

Duckworth, A. (2016). *Grit: The power of passion and perseverance*. Scribner.

Dweck, C. (2016). *Mindset: The new psychology of success*. Random House.

Ebersbach, M., Feierabend, M., & Nazari, K. B. B. (2020). Comparing the effects of generating questions, testing, and restudying on students' long-term recall in university learning. *Applied Cognitive Psychology, 34*(3), 640–656.

Finley, T. (2025, February 4). Scaffolding like a pro: Powerful ways to support learning. *Edutopia.* https://www.edutopia.org/article/powerful-scaffolding-strategies-support-learning/

Flavell, J. H. (1979). Metacognition and cognitive monitoring: A new area of cognitive–developmental inquiry. *American Psychologist, 34*(10), 906–911.

Freese, A. (2023). *Meant for more: Real talk about classrooms built on dignity, authenticity, and connection.* Solution Tree.

Frey, N., Hattie, J., & Fisher, D. (2018). *Developing assessment-capable visible learners, Grades K–12: Maximizing skill, will, and thrill.* Corwin.

Gaddi, N. R. (2025, March 6). From deep dives to skim reading: Students' decreasing attention spans. *The Whitman Wire.* https://whitmanwire.com/opinion/2025/03/06/from-deep-dives-to-skim-reading-students-decreasing-attention-spans/

González Jurado-Gutiérrez, G. (2024, December 8). Learning from trying: Challenging the stigmatisation of failure. *Telefónica.* https://www.telefonica.com/en/communication-room/blog/learning-challenging-stigmatisation-failure/

Hammond, Z. (2015). *Culturally responsive teaching and the brain: Promoting authentic engagement and rigor among culturally and linguistically diverse students.* Corwin.

Hammond, Z. (2024a, July 8). *Teaching for instructional equity and cognitive justice: Closing the knowing-doing gap* [Keynote address]. Annual Visible Learning Conference, San Diego, CA, United States.

Hammond, Z. (2024b, October 16). *Leveraging the science of reading for liberatory education* [Keynote presentation]. The Reading League Conference, Charlotte, NC, United States.

Hargrave, M., Fisher, D., & Frey, N. (2025). *Artificial intelligence playbook: Time-saving tools for teachers that make learning more . . . engaging* (2nd ed.). Corwin.

Hattie, J. (n.d.a). *Parental expectations* [Data set] (Visible Learning MetaX Version 1.3). https://www.visiblelearningmetax.com/influences/view/parental_expectations

Hattie, J. (n.d.b). *Self-reported grades* [Data set] (Visible Learning MetaX Version 1.3). https://www.visiblelearningmetax.com/influences/view/self-reported_grades

Hattie, J. (n.d.c). *Teacher clarity* [Data set] (Visible Learning MetaX Version 1.3). https://www.visiblelearningmetax.com/influences/view/teacher_clarity

Hattie, J. (n.d.d). *Teacher estimates of achievement* [Data set] (Visible Learning MetaX Version 1.3). https://www.visiblelearningmetax.com/influences/view/teacher_estimates_of_achievement_

Hattie, J. (n.d.e). *Teacher expectations* [Data set] (Visible Learning MetaX Version 1.3). https://www.visiblelearningmetax.com/influences/view/teacher_expectations

Hattie, J. (2012). *Visible learning for teachers: Maximizing impact on learning.* Routledge.

Hattie, J. (2020). *Visible learning: The power of intentional technology integration.* Routledge.

Hattie, J. (2023). *Visible learning: The sequel.* Corwin.

Hattie, J., Fisher, D., Frey, N., & Almarode, J. (2024). *The illustrated guide to visible learning: An introduction to what works best in schools.* Corwin.

Hattie, J., Fisher, D., Frey, N., & Clarke, S. (2021). *Collective student efficacy: Developing independent and inter-dependent learners.* Corwin.

Hattie, J., & Zierer, K. (2018). *10 mindframes for visible learning: Teaching for success.* Corwin.

Hollins-Alexander, S., & Law, N. V. (2022). *Collective equity: A movement for creating communities where we all can breathe.* Corwin.

Holt, J. (1983). *How children learn* (Rev. ed.). Delacorte Press.

Hubbard, F. (2023). *The equity expression: 6 entry points for nonnegotiable academic success.* Corwin.

Jensen, E. (2000). *Music with the brain in mind.* Corwin.

Johnson, D. W., & Johnson, R. T. (2009). *An educational psychology success story: Social interdependence theory and cooperative learning. Educational Researcher, 38*(5), 365–379. https://doi.org/10.3102/0013189X09339057

Jordan, A., & Hawley, T. (2012, January). Developing purpose based learning in U.S. history. *Ohio Social Studies Review,* 49, 18–55.

Kells, D. (2008). *The impact of music on language & early literacy*. Kindermusik. https://media2.kindermusik.com/website/2016/11/Research_Schools_Kindermusik_Impact-of-MM-on-Language-Early-Literacy_2016.pdf

Kurczek, J., & Johnson, J. (2014). The student as teacher: Reflections on collaborative learning in a senior seminar. *Journal of Undergraduate Neuroscience Education,* 44(6), 937–958.

Lara-Alecio, R., Tong, F., Irby, B. J., Guerrero, C., Huerta, M., & Fan, Y. (2012). The effect of an instructional intervention on middle school English learners' science and English reading achievement. *Journal of Research in Science Teaching,* 49(8), 987–1011. https://doi.org/10.1002/tea.21031

Leh, K. (2025). SEL competencies and skills. <Poster>. Copyright 2020 by CASEL.

McSpadden, K. (2015, May 14). Science: You now have a shorter attention span than a goldfish. *Time*. https://time.com/3858309/attention-spans-goldfish/

Minor, C. (2019). *We got this: Equity, access, and the quest to be who our students need us to be*. Heinemann.

Murayama, K., & Elliot, A. J. (2009). The joint influence of personal achievement goals and classroom goal structures on achievement-relevant outcomes. *Journal of Educational Psychology, 101*(2), 432–447.

National Center for Education Statistics. (2024, May). High school graduation rates. *Condition of education*. U.S. Department of Education. https://nces.ed.gov/programs/coe/indicator/coi/high-school-graduation-rates

The New Teacher Project (TNTP). (2018). *The opportunity myth: What students can show us about how school is letting them down—And how to fix it*. https://tntp.org/publication/the-opportunity-myth/

Nordengren, C. (2022). *Step into student goal setting: A path to growth, motivation, and agency*. Corwin.

Nowik, O. (2025, June 1). These 10 things will happen when you start stepping out of your comfort zone. *LifeHack*. https://www.lifehack.org/291049/these-10-things-will-happen-when-you-start-stepping-out-you-comfort-zone

Peterson, E. R., Sharma, T., Bird, A., E Henderson, A. M., Ramgopal, V., Reese, E., & B. Morton, S. M. (2024). How mothers talk to their children about failure, mistakes and setbacks is related to their children's fear of failure. *British Journal of Educational Psychology,* 95(1), 124.

Prendergast, L., & Lee, P. (2024). *Habits of resilient educators: Strategies for thriving during times of anxiety, doubt, and constant change*. Corwin.

Prendergast, L., & Lee, P. (2025). *Habits of resilient leaders: Personal practices that drive professional impact*. Corwin.

Ritchhart, R. (2023). *8 questions to drive a culture of thinking*. Cultures of Thinking in Action.

Rubie-Davies, C. (2014). *Becoming a high-expectation teacher: Raising the bar*. Routledge.

Saleebey, D. (Ed.). (2013). *The strengths perspective in social work practice* (6th ed.). Pearson. Samuels, C. A. (2020, September 2). GreatSchools' ratings revamp, credits schools for boosting academic growth. *Education Week*. https://www.edweek.org/policy-politics/greatschools-ratings-revamp-credits-schools-for-boosting-academic-growth/2020/09

Smith, D., Fisher, D., & Frey, N. (2024, October 1). *What does it mean to be "supported" in school?* Corwin Connect.

Southwick, S. M., & Charney, D. S. (2018). *Resilience: The science of mastering life's greatest challenges* (2nd ed.). Cambridge University Press.

Stiggins, R. J., Arter, J. A., Chappuis, J., & Chappuis, S. (2006). *Classroom assessment for student learning: Doing it right—Using it well*. Pearson Assessment Training Institute.

Stone, D., & Heen, S. (2014). *Thanks for the feedback: The science and art of receiving feedback well*. Viking.

Sweeney, D., & Harris, L. S. (2017). *Student-centered coaching: The moves*. Corwin.

Tomlinson, C. A. (2017). *How to differentiate instruction in academically diverse classrooms* (3rd ed.). ACSD.

U.S. Department of Education. (2023). *Chronic absenteeism*. https://www.ed.gov/teaching-and-administration/supporting-students/chronic-absenteeism

Walsh, J. A., & Sattes, B. D. (2017). *Quality questioning: Research-based practice to engage every learner*. Corwin.

Wellman, B., & Lipton, L. (2024). *Data-driven dialogue: A facilitator's guide to collaborative inquiry* (2nd ed.). Solution Tree.

Wilhelm, J. D., & Smith, M. W. (2014). Reading don't fix no Chevys (yet!) Motivating boys in the age of the common core. *Journal of Adolescent & Adult Literacy, 58*(4), 273–276. https://doi.org/10.1002/jaal.361

World Economic Forum. (2020). *Future of jobs report 2023*. https://www.weforum.org/publications/the-future-of-jobs-report-2023/

Yeager, D. (2024). *10 to 25: The science of motivating young people: A groundbreaking approach to leading the next generation—And making your own life easier*. Simon & Schuster.

Yeager, D., & Dweck, C. (2020). What can be learned from growth mindset controversies? *American Psychologist, 75*(9), 1269–1284.

Zohar, A., & Barzilai, S. (2013). A review of research on metacognition in science education: Current and future directions. *Studies in Science Education, 49*(2), 121–169.

Index